INSIDE
unREAL
ESTATE

INSIDE unREAL ESTATE

A JOURNEY THROUGH INDIA'S MOST CONTROVERSIAL SECTOR

Sushil Kumar Sayal

Foreword by
Sunil Bharti Mittal

PORTFOLIO
PENGUIN

An imprint of Penguin Random House

PORTFOLIO

USA | Canada | UK | Ireland | Australia
New Zealand | India | South Africa | China | Singapore

Portfolio is part of the Penguin Random House group of companies
whose addresses can be found at global.penguinrandomhouse.com

Published by Penguin Random House India Pvt. Ltd
4th Floor, Capital Tower 1, MG Road,
Gurugram 122 002, Haryana, India

Penguin
Random House
India

First published in Portfolio by Penguin Books India 2016

10 9 8 7 6 5 4 3 2

ISBN 9780670088522

Typeset in Dante MT Std by Manipal Digital Systems, Manipal
Printed at Replika Press Pvt. Ltd, India

www.penguin.co.in

This is a legitimate digitally printed version of the book and therefore might not
have certain extra finishing on the cover.

To my father, Girdhari Lal Sayal (1936–2013)

Contents

Acknowledgements

Some years ago, I happened to read Stephen R. Covey's groundbreaking book, *The 7 Habits of Highly Effective People*. The book left a lasting impression on me. What I found truly amazing was the way Covey integrated his personal experiences and observations with managerial and behavioural lessons.

The book was first published in 1989 and has sold more than fifteen million copies worldwide in thirty-eight languages. When I finished reading the book, I realized that by using simple measures we can enhance our output. From that day onwards, I have regarded Covey as my management guru. Born in 1932, he was a businessman, educator and intellectual. Regarded as one of the foremost thinkers of our times, Covey died in 2012 at the age of seventy-nine.

The seven habits that he identified, which can truly transform your life, are:

Be proactive,

Begin with the end in mind,

Put first things first,

Think win-win,

Seek to understand before you are understood,

Synergize,

And balance your resources, health and energy to create a sustainable, effective lifestyle.

Just the way Dale Carnegie impacted generations of people world over with his simple message in *How to Win Friends and Influence People*, Covey touched the lives of millions who are constantly looking for ways to do better. I happen to be one of them. I think the reason why humans exist is to learn and improve all the time. Those who fail to reinvent themselves lose out in life.

Apart from Covey, I deeply acknowledge the role played by several colleagues in my career. When I was still young in the industry, there were some people who took me under their wing. From them, I learnt the dignity of labour and the need to look at things from a long-term perspective. Had it not been for their timely intervention, my life would have taken a different path altogether. I thank my stars that during the better part of my career, I got to work with businessmen and companies that placed ethics and honesty above everything else. These qualities, fortunately for me, quickly became a part of my DNA.

I am grateful to my parents for inculcating in me the values of honesty and hard work. Their emphasis on education came very handy in life. I am also grateful to my wife, Kanika Sayal, my daughter, Aayushi, her better half, Samarth, and my son, Ankush, for their support and love. Without their constant encouragement, this book would not have been possible.

A word of thanks to my friends Harsimron Sandhu and Aman Sood for their help, and also to Bhupesh Bhandari for his friendly advice. I would also like to thank my commissioning editor at Penguin Random House, Lohit Jagwani, for his infectious enthusiasm and sharp observations. I am grateful for the way he helped give shape to my thoughts.

Foreword

In his book *Inside unReal Estate*, Sushil Kumar Sayal, who has spent over three decades in the real estate sector, gives an insider's view of the ever-evolving dynamics of the property market space in India.

His first-hand account of the complexities in the sector—where necessity coexists with luxury and affordability with opulence—gives useful insights into the challenges in developing housing for all.

Going by estimates, by 2030, 500 million people will be living in cities. This would require 800–1000 million square metres of residential and commercial space. This space would have to be built keeping in mind the aspirations of 'young' India—more aware of its rights as well as its obligations.

Today, the challenge of urbanization is being addressed through progressive initiatives by the government. 'Smart Cities' and 'Digital India' have opened up new avenues for investment that would also contribute to growth and help provide jobs. As we build our towns and cities, we have to make informed choices to achieve the desired trade-offs and build sustainable cities.

Preface

Indian real estate—can one ever say enough about it? The sector is vibrant with ceaseless transformation, innovation and activity. It is also a hard, demanding taskmaster. Many venture into it with stars in their eyes, but very few make a significant mark in the field. Success smiles only at those with above-average insight and acumen—at those people with progressive vision, uncommon courage and zeal.

The story of Indian real estate is worthy of a book—several books, in fact. Truth to be told, an entire encyclopedia would be required to cover all its facets and manifestations. To say that such an exercise would be a tedious one to take up is an understatement. What is doable is a book which talks of the companies and people who have given the Indian real estate sector the form and shape it has today.

India's real estate market does have its heroes. These people were able to observe the larger picture, and then they proceeded to add their own indelible brushstrokes to the canvas. What differentiated them from their contemporaries was a deep understanding of what makes this sector tick. They accepted the overall scenario with all its flaws, loopholes and inconsistencies, harnessed their resources and bravely put them on the line.

And this is the foundation of every success story. While many recognize the amazing potential of the Indian real estate sector, few are willing to go all the way in helping shape its direction and, thereby, its future. To carve a niche in this highly unorganized business arena is comparable to building on shifting desert sands—impossible for most, yet those who succeed leave monumental pyramids in their wake.

In penning this book, Sushil Kumar Sayal has rendered a valuable service to the sector. The living legends of this dynamic field come to life within its pages, and he has drawn generously from his own experiences over several years. I commend him for writing this exemplary book, which has obviously taken a long time to complete. I am confident that this work will set a new benchmark in literature, and I look forward to more such offerings from his fertile pen.

Anuj Puri,
chairman and country head, JLL India

INSIDE
unREAL
ESTATE

Introduction

Zar, Zoru, Zameen

'Buy land, they are not making it anymore.'
—*Mark Twain*

There is an old saying in northern India that three factors are at the root of all conflict: *zar*, *zoru* and *zameen* (gold, woman and land). Wars have been fought over the three from time immemorial. These have been the cause of much of the fratricide we see in history and have led to innumerable families being torn asunder. In modern times, it is often said that behind most controversies is zameen—land or real estate.

It may be embroiled in scams and scandals, but land is a highly sensitive issue in India. That's why emotions run high every time the issue of taking farm land away from cultivators for commercial or industrial purposes comes up. It is seen as a grand conspiracy to deprive the farmers of their only possession. Naturally, this is an issue that political parties just don't want to let go off as farmers make up a large chunk of the vote bank.

There's a reason why Indians are so emotional about real estate. For several generations, we have been taught that our first investment should always be a house: a roof over one's head. Everything else can wait. Apart from education, it is the single possession that Indians value the most. A man who doesn't own a house is seen as incomplete or poor.

From the long-term perspective, almost all Indians see it as the safest investment. Not just in India, wherever Indians go in the world, they quickly emerge as the movers and shakers of the property market: London, New York, Singapore, Dubai.

Because it is perceived as precious—the ultimate security against life's unforeseen contingencies—and because it has been grossly unregulated, it is also one of the most maligned sectors of the economy; the breeding ground for a million scandals.

The thought of writing this book occurred to me some time back when I realized that the whole sector had—unfairly—a very bad reputation. Everybody, whether perfectly honest or a crook, was painted with the same brush.

I would hear other industries talk with pride about their high ethical practices, stringent governance and absolute transparency; why, I would wonder, weren't the country's real estate barons talking about such things? Not everything was rotten in this sector.

There was good reason for it: nobody, including the common man, was prepared to believe that the business of real estate could be carried out in a clean and transparent way. I felt that somebody had to set the record straight.

At the end of the day, real estate development is a business like any other. Why should its rules and moral standards be different? Having always played by the rules, I felt it was important to tell my story; a journey of over three decades, where things got done only the way they should.

I also felt that the negative publicity around the sector should not deter youngsters from entering the field. India today produces some of the finest young talent in the world, but many of them choose to steer clear of real estate. Unless they are told that this sector, too, can be clean and free of manipulation, it will never be able to attract fresh talent.

Real estate as a sector is constantly evolving, though the changes may be slow. The big leap came when humans moved from caves to houses. Then in 1853, when Elisha Otis invented the elevator, construction began to grow vertically. It became possible for people to live in high-rise buildings. Had it not been for Otis, the world would not have seen skyscrapers. This contribution to human civilization needs to be appreciated.

The recent drive in India for smart cities is another step in this direction. Through smart constructions and information technology, the whole look and feel of habitats will change. Lifestyles will improve. Chores will become less burdensome. The quality of life will go up.

The contribution of builders in wealth creation has always been grossly overlooked. Those who bought houses twenty or even ten years ago have seen a huge appreciation in their net worth. Real estate, I felt, needed an authoritative book to point out these factors. Somebody had to tell the full story—faults and all.

But, I have to concede that there is a lot of merit to the popular perception that real estate is a cesspool of corruption and irregularities. This fact cannot be brushed under the carpet. It cannot be wished away.

One of the factors that brought disrepute to the Congress-led United Progressive Alliance, and played no small role in its ouster in the May 2014 general elections, was the Adarsh Housing Society scam in which the high and mighty—politicians, bureaucrats and senior armed forces personnel—conspired to bag prime real estate in south Mumbai at throwaway prices.

The flats were meant for war widows and defence personnel, but the powers that be conspired to twist the rules and apportioned these at rates way below the market price.

In the infamous telecom spectrum scam, two of the alleged conspirators happened to be real estate tycoons. The real estate angle was talked about in the murder of a senior bureaucrat in Karnataka.

Right through the first few months of 2014, when he was in the thick of his campaign to become the prime minister of the country, Narendra Modi was accused by his opponents of giving away land to Gautam Adani, a businessman he is supposedly close to, virtually free when he was the chief minister of Gujarat.

It was contested by Modi, as well as Adani, that the land was unfit for agricultural use and was, therefore, sold at a low price. Also, large tracts of it was awarded to Adani when the Congress was in power in the state.

Likewise, the Congress government in Haryana, which was decimated in the 2014 state elections, came under fire for speedily mutating the land use agreement in the state so that Robert Vadra—a member of the country's most prominent political family—could sell the large tracts of real estate he allegedly owned to a builder and book profits. This too snowballed into a huge issue during the general elections, though it must be said that no charge of impropriety on Vadra's part has been proven so far.

Even the country's venerated armed forces have not remained untouched by land scams. A top-ranking officer was removed from service after a court inquiry found him guilty of transferring land adjacent to a military station near Siliguri in West Bengal to a private builder in 2008.

Special economic zones, which were meant to boost manufacturing in the country, ended up becoming just land that could be diverted for other purposes.

The extent of black money that gets generated in real estate is huge, which in these times of heightened public awareness is unsustainable. In the last few years, there has been a strong demand to bring back all the black money Indians have taken out of the country, though nobody—not even the government—has any idea how much is stashed away and how can it be brought back.

The Bharatiya Janata Party's claim in the run up to the 2014 general elections that it would bring back all the black money abroad within 100 days of coming to power has remained just a promise on paper.

What people forget is that a large part of it is in the country, in the open—invested in real estate. It is there for all to see.

Towards the end of 2014, Yadav Singh, then the chief engineer of Noida, Greater Noida and Yamuna Expressway (as chief engineer, he had the authority to approve public projects of up to Rs. 1 crore), was under investigation by the income tax department. The sleuths reportedly recovered expensive cars, Rs. 15 crore stashed away in an SUV parked outside his house, diamonds worth Rs. 100 crore, 2 kg of gold jewellery and papers that suggested he owned several properties.

Till a court of law decides on the matter, these will remain just allegations, but it could well be yet another instance of black money finding its way into real estate. In most corruption cases, the property sector features prominently.

A few days before the Singh affair came into the spotlight, Cobrapost, the investigative website, had disclosed the findings of a sting operation code-named Black Ninja.

'In an investigation lasting more than eighteen months, Cobrapost found thirty-five real estate companies with a pan-India presence across nine states willing to do bulk transactions in black money. These companies admit helping their clients convert black money into white by letting them pay in cash a substantial part of the sale price of the properties they buy, in blatant violation of Income Tax laws, Foreign Exchange Management Act, Prevention of Money Laundering Act and other laws. The black money component in these deals ranges from 10 per cent to 90 per cent. In one instance, a developer's employee was even willing to accept Rs. 100 crore in black money,' it said in a press release.

'Senior officials said that accepting payments in black was nothing new for them and that it was an accepted norm of the real estate industry. They were willing to accept hard cash in any city and even abroad, through hawala. Some were ready to sell a property before all mandatory approvals are attained, knowing fully well that this is illegal. A senior executive of a company suggests depositing the entire component of the deal in a bank account which will be closed as soon as it is credited,' it added.

It is an open secret that payment in cash is the norm in the secondary market; the Cobrapost investigation showed the practice is just as prevalent in the primary market as well. It also gave the layperson an idea of how it has become a medium to convert black money into white.

According to Liases Foras, a real estate consultancy, about 30 per cent of all property transactions in 2012 used black money. As real estate is about a tenth of the Indian economy, the extent of black money floating around in the sector is huge—many times more than what is said to be locked in vaults abroad.

Black money in the secondary real estate market has become almost impossible to track. In cities, there is a circle rate which is used as a ready reckoner by the authorities for tax purposes. If the sale price is higher than the circle rate, there is an incentive for the seller to underdeclare the payment, which means that the disclosed price is below the actual transaction value he declares—that the sale price was the same as the circle rate, allowing him to accept a large chunk of the payment in cash, thus saving on tax.

So, it makes sense to fix the circle rate as close to the market price as possible. But there is a flip side to it: a high circle rate reduces the scope for price correction when the market enters a downturn—like it did in 2014. Areas where the rates fell below the circle rate saw all transactions coming to a standstill.

To curb black money in the primary market, the government has made it mandatory for all buyers to quote their permanent account number in all transactions. But buyers have got round this rule by using multiple accounts. Fraudsters always find ways to stay a step ahead of the law.

In an interview to *Mint* in December 2014, finance minister Arun Jaitley said that the government is looking to link all real estate transactions with Aadhar, the unique identity number. Such a move could indeed bring some transparency in the real estate market.

More was on the anvil. In his 2015–16 Union budget speech, delivered on 28 February 2015, Jaitley said he plans to introduce a revamped version of the lapsed Benami Transactions (Prohibition) Bill soon in Parliament. 'This law,' he said, 'will enable confiscation of *benami* property and provide for prosecution, thus blocking a major avenue for generation and holding of black money in the form of benami property, especially in real estate.'

For the uninitiated, benami means anonymous and the motive of such deals is to hide the identity of the true buyer or seller.

Mistaking the parking of black money in real estate as genuine demand from home buyers, many developers overbuilt in the last few years. As a result, by 2014, it was clear that most real estate markets were sitting on massive inventories.

According to Liases Foras data quoted in newspaper reports, Delhi and its suburbs were sitting on an inventory of eighty-three months at the end of September 2014. In simple words, it would take Delhi and its suburbs almost seven years to sell their current stock of unsold homes, going by the current pace of sales. In Mumbai and Chennai, the inventory would take fifty months to clear. In Bangalore, it was forty-one months; and in Hyderabad, thirty-eight months. There was a glut in the market.

The prevalence of black money has ensured that real estate prices stay extremely high, despite the country's low per capita income.

According to one study, it will take an Indian, with the average per capita income, 580 years to buy a top-end property in Mumbai, compared to sixty-five years in Hong Kong, sixty-two years in Paris and forty-seven years in New York. A report that appeared in *Business Standard* in August 2015 said, citing real estate consultants, that only double-income households could afford to buy a decent-sized flat (a 2 BHK with 1000 square feet of super built-up area) in India's top eight cities—and the list did not include Mumbai.

You will find it hard to come across another sector where so many things have gone wrong.

Builders delay projects with impunity. There have been instances when builders have simply vanished with the money they collected from the buyers. A sizeable number of new contractors are just fly-by-night operators. Hundreds of thousands of hapless buyers have lost their hard-earned money to unscrupulous realtors.

Buying a house has always been the top priority of every Indian (the demand for housing really exploded after the government offered income tax benefits for the sector). Buyers often work really hard and make innumerable sacrifices just for the security of living in their own homes. But the dream has turned sour for many, thanks to errant builders.

The contract between the builder and buyer is opaque and filled with legalese. More often than not, the buyer fails to read the fine print and pays dearly for this oversight.

There is also no uniform definition of built-up area, covered area, super area, carpet area et cetera, which leads to buyers frequently being short-changed by builders.

Some time back, an elderly Sikh gentleman met me in my office. He was a retired army officer and had invested all his savings in a commercial property. But the builder gave him something totally different—something much inferior—from what he had been promised. The man was shattered, to say the least. It was clear that he would never trust a builder again. One could say he was naïve to trust the builder with his hard-earned money, but then if most builders are cheats, who do you trust?

Construction laws are openly flouted as dishonest builders collude with corrupt bureaucrats. In fact, I am convinced that bureaucrats deliberately keep the rules complex. This is rent-seeking by another name. If all the procedures are simplified, they will be left with no discretionary power. And nobody wants to give up power—and the money that comes with it.

Some states have talked of single-window clearances, but the ground reality is completely different.

Not for nothing did a 2013 survey by Ernst & Young and the Federation of Indian Chambers of Commerce and Industry say infrastructure and real estate is perceived as the most corrupt sector of the economy.

The corruption affects the entire supply chain. In a market like Gurgaon, black money adds 10 to 20 per cent to the land cost. And since land accounts for 30 to 50 per cent of the project cost, this black money escalates overall cost by 3 to 10 per cent. But this is hardly a cost that the builder absorbs: He recovers each and every paisa of this money from unsuspecting customers.

In other words, money is taken out of the pockets of the buyers and put into the pockets of corrupt bureaucrats and their middlemen—after the builder has kept his cut. If a leader says this doesn't happen, surely he doesn't know the truth or he chooses to ignore it.

Every day, newer ways in which builders dupe buyers emerge. One ploy many builders use is to build extra floors. This can have dire consequences.

Think of a buyer who has bought an apartment in a ten-floor block. His decision to purchase a house in this project is based on the assumption that he will share the common infrastructure with residents of ten floors. Midway, the builder decides to add ten more floors. The buyer's assumption goes haywire: He now has to share the infrastructure with twice the number of people. This is completely unfair to the buyer.

Of course, the builder needs to take the permission of the authorities, which seldom seems to be denied. A bigger example of the collusion between business and government than the builder–bureaucrat nexus will be hard to find.

Moreover, when the builder builds a ten-floor block, he digs the foundation to a certain depth; when the additional floors are added, does he ensure the foundation is deeper? He doesn't. The authorities not only turn a blind eye to this safety hazard but are often hand in glove with errant builders. Will this be permitted in any developed country? Certainly not.

This is what seems to have happened in the Campa Cola Compound at Worli in Mumbai.

In the early 1980s, Pure Drinks, which used to make the Campa Cola aerated beverage, gave the rights to three builders— Yusuf Patel, B.K. Gupta and PSB Construction Company—to build residential flats in the allocated land in Worli. The builders constructed more flats than the number they were permitted to and sold them to unsuspecting buyers.

Most of the buyers didn't know something was amiss. Those who raised questions were told that that sanction from the Brihanmumbai Municipal Corporation, or BMC, would come shortly with the payment of a nominal fine.

Indeed, BMC did issue stop-work notices to the builders; in return, they paid penalties and resumed work. When the flats were constructed, nobody from BMC or any other arm of the government prevented the buyers from occupying these flats.

After a protracted legal battle, the Supreme Court in June 2014 sanctioned the demolition of the extra constructions. About 100 flat-owners were affected. Where would these people go? Many of them were rendered homeless.

Or take the example of the Allahabad High Court's order to demolish two residential high-rises in Supertech Emerald Court in Noida.

The Residents' Welfare Association of Emerald Court had filed a petition in the court that the builder had raised the towers from twenty-four floors to forty floors 'without maintaining the mandatory distance of sixteen metres from the adjoining block', which had made the buildings unsafe and also blocked out air and light.

Supertech, the builder, argued that all relevant permissions from the Noida Authority were taken and said it would challenge the verdict in a higher court. The decision was upheld by the Supreme Court.

If the builder was at fault, so were the officials who cleared the files. But one has not heard of any action being taken against them.

Other malpractices too have come to light. In May 2014, a famous builder and two members of his family were all arrested by the Gurgaon Police, for cheating over 700 investors. The police, news reports suggested, claimed the fraud was to the tune of Rs. 1000 crore.

In another case, the Competition Appellate Tribunal upheld a penalty of over Rs. 600 crore imposed on DLF, undoubtedly the country's biggest builder, by the Competition Commission of India. In May 2010, the Belaire Owners' Association had complained against DLF before the Competition Commission that the builder had 'imposed highly arbitrary, unfair and unreasonable conditions on the apartment allottees of the housing complex, The Belaire, which has serious adverse effects and ramifications on the rights of the allottees'. In August 2011, the Competition Commission of India found DLF violating fair trade norms and imposed a fine of Rs. 630 crore on it.

'This certainly was not a fight between equals. We are also not unmindful of the fact that any individual, howsoever rich he may be, after investing crores of rupees, could not have quit the scheme, in view of the fact that he had become a trapped customer. The order of the Competition Commission as well as this judgment is expected to go a long way to ameliorate all the conditions of the customers,' the Competition Appellate Tribunal said in its judgement.

'Competition law must be read in the light of the philosophy of the Constitution of India, which has concern for the consumers. If the consumer is exploited by a mighty builder, then such mighty builder cannot claim soft attitude from the state,' it added.

Another builder in the suburbs of Delhi faced the wrath of his buyers for constructing a school in the middle of a gated community! The decision was taken without consulting the buyers. Naturally, they were up in arms against him.

Not just builders, but brokers too dupe buyers without pity or remorse. In fact, there is a close relationship between builders and brokers. Thus, very few builders in and around Delhi put their money into a project upfront. As soon as he wins land in an auction, he collects his band of brokers and sells the project to them. With that money, he pays for the land. The brokers, in return, are assured of space at a discount.

Since he has given a discount to the brokers, the builder overbuilds in order to make money. The extra construction is frequently regularized. Even if it isn't, nothing stops the builder and brokers from selling it. Often, the builder doesn't even bother to get a completion certificate.

What emboldens them is the rapidity with which illegal constructions get regularized. In an article in *Mint*, Swati Ramanathan, the chairperson of Jana Urban Space Foundation and co-founder of the Janaagraha Centre for Citizenship and Democracy, presented some startling statistics.

In Mumbai, between January 2012 and March 2013 alone, the municipal authorities received more than 21,000 complaints about unauthorized constructions. In addition, 55,000 buildings in the city were estimated to be occupied without the required certification.

In Delhi, four to five million people lived in 1,639 unauthorized colonies, including 200 of them on forest land and space that belonged to the Archaeological Survey of India. 'State regularization initiatives, unfortunately, have become tainted as tools for corruption or political populism, or as a means to generate revenue for the state,' Ramanathan wrote.

In Kolkata, she added, a meagre penalty of Rs. 500 per square feet allows regularization of illegal floors! It almost seems like an open invitation for all to flout the norms without fear.

Under the law, a builder cannot sell his project unless he has secured all the clearances. These clearances can take up to two years to obtain. Given the high land prices all over the country, no builder can afford to let the investment sit idle for two years. He has no choice but to violate the law and pre-sell the project.

Other irregularities too are rampant. The law requires all builders to put the money collected from buyers in an escrow account. That money cannot be used for any other purpose. This rule is also openly flouted.

It's no surprise that buyers have lost all faith in builders. There is, therefore, a massive trust deficit between builders, brokers and buyers.

Thanks to all these malpractices, especially the rampant black money, the country's top business houses till a few years ago rarely entered the sector. Their exposure to real estate, at best, was sporadic. Many of them found it difficult to handle this huge flow of unaccounted cash. It is only now that things have started to change and the corporatization of real estate has started in earnest.

The stock market has, for several years now, taken a dim view of builders. As a result, their share prices have crashed from the peaks they had scaled in 2008. DLF slipped from Rs. 350 in January 2010 to around Rs. 145 five years later. Unitech tumbled from Rs. 80 to Rs. 17 during the period. This is a serious erosion in value.

A report published by *Business Standard* in September 2015 found that most real estate barons saw their net worth melt down in the last few years. Between December 2007, when real estate valuations were at their peak, and 15 August 2015, K.P. Singh of DLF's net worth declined by 90.5 per cent. This was still better than Ramesh Chandra of Unitech (99.1 per cent), Ramesh Wadhawan of HDIL (93.2 per cent), Pradeep Jain and Sanjeev Jain of Parsvnath Developers (91.4 per cent) and Hemant Shah and Vyomesh Shah of Hubtown (91.1 per cent). In dollars, the report went to add, their net worth was down 95 per cent.

The investor sentiment is such that new builders find it impossible to raise money from the primary market. Banks are extremely cautious: They do not lend money to builders easily. As long as the market was buoyant, the banks opened their purse strings wholeheartedly for builders.

Typically, banks borrow at 10–12 per cent annual interest; as long as the builders promised them 15 per cent earnings, they turned a blind eye to all the malpractices prevalent in the sector. It was only when defaults began to happen, and the Reserve Bank of India raised an alarm over the sheer number of non-payments, they began to tighten the screws.

As the misdemeanours of the builders have begun to increase, buyers have been left with no option but to seek redressal from the courts.

With improved access to information, thanks to the Right to Information Act, and the rising anti-corruption sentiment in the country, buyers are becoming more vocal and better organized. Much of the judicial intervention has resulted from their activism.

There is evidence that one association of home buyers, which won a case against the contractor, is now training other associations on how to take errant builders to task.

In my career in real estate, I have come across numerous instances of irrational behaviour.

Many years ago, a relative called to say that somebody he knew was in great distress, and requested my assistance. I agreed to meet the man and help him.

He was in his early thirties. That he was in some sort of emotional pain was very evident by the fact that there were tears in his eyes. His story was sad but not an unusual one. The man ran a business in Chandni Chowk in Old Delhi. Along with his father and brothers, he was a wholesale seller of *lungis* and the family had been running this business for nearly four decades now. It was doing reasonably well. The family was comfortably placed in life, but not fabulously rich. One day, his brother-in-law came home with a proposition that turned his life around.

His brother-in-law had the reputation of being lazy; however, he was now doing fairly well. That's because he had entered the property business in Gurgaon, the boom town coming up in the outskirts of Delhi. He would buy flats and plots and sell them at a premium. He was turning money around quickly and making a handsome profit in the bargain.

The man was tempted. The lungi business was steady, but not spectacular. It would not have made him very rich. He realized that even if he spent a decade in his family's business, he would never make the kind of money his brother-in-law made in a single year.

He decided to join hands with his brother-in-law. The partnership got off to a tremendous start. On his brother-in-law's advice, he began to buy and sell properties. Over the next one-and-a-half years, he made huge profits—amounts he couldn't even dream of in his family's business.

The stories of his success and new wealth began to spread in Chandni Chowk. Many of his acquaintances offered to place their money at his disposal in the hope that he would be able to double it. He finally took money from about twenty-five people.

Now that he had more money at his disposal, the man's deals started to get bigger and bigger. He started getting noticed in the market. Sellers and brokers started approaching him in droves.

One day, he was approached by somebody who said that a piece of property allotted to a doctor was up for sale. It was located on Golf Course Road, Gurgaon's prime market, and was available cheap: The seller was asking for just Rs. 7 crore.

The man fell for it. He put in Rs. 2 crore himself and for the remaining Rs. 5 crore, he went back to his acquaintances and associates in Chandni Chowk.

Those people had no reason to mistrust him. After all, he was the man with the Midas touch. They gave him the money and he bought the property.

But the property was earmarked for a hospital (such real estate is usually allotted at a subsidized rate; in return, the hospitals agree to treat a fixed number of poor patients free of cost). It could not be converted into a block of apartments or a shopping mall. As a result, the authorities cancelled the allotment and confiscated the land. A large chunk of the Rs. 7 crore paid by the man was in cash, which meant there was no official record of money changing hands. There was no way he could have recovered this money from the seller.

The man was finished. He met all the authorities, including the chief minister of Haryana, but all his efforts came to naught. Meanwhile, the investors were baying for his blood. They had camped at his father's home and were refusing to leave unless their money was returned in full.

As a result, the family's lungi business too took a beating. He stopped going to Chandni Chowk altogether, perhaps out of shame as well as fear, and had attempted suicide not once but thrice.

The man was blinded by the windfall profits he had made in the last one year. So much so, he forgot to do the basic due diligence, and paid dearly for this oversight.

But this is a regular fallout of all bullish markets—valuations rise so steeply and the thought of quick profits eclipses reasonable behaviour.

During the early years of this century, there was a similar rush with regard to internet companies. Private equity funds and other high net worth investors rushed into the sector, even though the business models were half-baked.

Such was the lure of multiplying investments that all established due diligence norms were forgotten. Deals were, at times, struck in under an hour. When the dotcom boom went bust, a lot of people were left with absolutely nothing.

This herd mentality shows that not many people understand the dynamics of the market. There is, therefore, a great need to demystify the real estate sector.

At the moment, investing in real estate is fraught with great risks: buyers have little idea if the land titles are clear, various clearances have been received or not, and what is the track record of the builder.

There is no agency that rates real estate projects: what is the probability of the project being delivered on time and according to the agreed-upon specifications. The problem is that such transparency will drive a lot of people out of business. There are vested interests that want this opacity to continue.

It is no surprise that the sector suffers from a serious image problem. Throughout the pre-liberalization days, business in general, and builders in particular, were shown in popular culture as crooks who would stop at nothing to make a quick profit.

While the perception of businessmen has undergone some change, that of builders remains the same. In *Khosla ka Ghosla*, the 2006 film directed by Dibakar Banerjee, actor Boman Irani portrays the 'typical' builder: manipulative, unprincipled and somewhat unsophisticated.

Not just real estate—the lack of ethics in Indian business is well known. Seldom does one come across a company or a businessman who doesn't mind paying his way through the various clearances required. Cronyism has earned Indian business a bad name.

In his 2012 book, *Breakout Nations*, Ruchir Sharma said that any country that produces too many billionaires, relative to its size, is in all likelihood off balance. 'If the average billionaire of a country has amassed too much wealth, not just billions but tens of billions, the lack of balance can lead to stagnation,' he wrote.

At that time, he had said that 'many of India's super rich still inspire national pride, not resentment, and they can travel the country with no fear for their safety', but this 'genial state of affairs could change quickly'.

The country may have well reached this point. The governor of the Reserve Bank of India, Raghuram Rajan, in July 2014, came down heavily on crony capitalism—the nexus between 'corrupt businessmen' and 'venal' and 'corrupt politicians'—which, he said, is 'killing transparency and competition' and is 'harmful to free enterprise, opportunity and economic growth'.

The 2014 general elections saw a larger discussion on this issue. 'If the debate during the elections is any pointer, this is a very real concern of the public in India today,' Rajan added.

One school of thought says that Japan and South Korea progressed rapidly because a handful of their companies were singled out for special treatment by the government, and they delivered the results. Most of them have become global conglomerates.

That may be true but the Indian experience inspires no confidence. What did some new telecom companies do when the government gave them inexpensive spectrum? At least two of them sold their stakes to foreigners at a huge premium. It was only after the Comptroller and Auditor General quantified the loss—to the tune of Rs. 1.76 lakh crore—that the people came to know the extent of the scam.

Similarly, the special economic zones became an opportunity for land grabbing. And coal blocks were undervalued and acquired by private companies.

These instances shouldn't surprise anybody because cronyism has been an integral part of Indian business. In the pre-liberalization age, many business houses got industrial licences and just sat on them in order to create a scarcity which would keep prices high.

Most worked behind the scenes to ensure that rivals were denied licences. 'An important issue in the recent election was whether we had substituted crony socialism of the past with crony capitalism where the rich and the influential are alleged to have received land, natural resources and spectrum in return for payoffs to venal politicians,' Rajan had added.

Cronyism acts as a major barrier affecting entry into regulated businesses. It is not easy to take on established players who have the decision-makers on their payrolls. If they can pressure the central government to transfer those ministers who do not cater to their interests, imagine the damage they can inflict on newcomers.

That's why most young entrepreneurs these days are happy to confine themselves to unregulated sectors like information technology.

One way to end cronyism in the allocation of natural resources is to ensure there are transparent auctions. So far, it seems to have worked well, as was seen in the second round of spectrum and coal auctions. There is no reason why it can't be replicated in other sectors. The government also needs to put in place safeguards which will ensure that there is no collusion between the bidders.

So strong is popular resentment against cronyism and private sector corruption that nobody has dared to name a businessman for a Bharat Ratna for some time now. The last such demand was made almost twelve years ago when the then telecom minister Pramod Mahajan said Dhirubhai Ambani should be given the award. When the Bharat Ratna could be given to *nachnewale* and *ganewale* (dancers and singers), why not the businessman, he had asked.

Soon after his comment, Atal Bihari Vajpayee, the then prime minister, dropped Mahajan from the cabinet and asked him to work for the party as a general secretary.

Many people often try to confuse cronyism with lobbying. Conceptually, there is nothing wrong with lobbying. Businessmen, like anybody else, have every right to lobby with the elected representatives for what they think is good for them. But the line between lobbying and cronyism is a very thin one.

Still, there are winds of change. The Union cabinet in April 2015 gave its nod to set up a real estate regulator. This will have far-reaching consequences for investors in commercial as well as residential property.

In 2014, the Securities and Exchange Board of India, or SEBI, gave its approval for real estate investment trusts, or REITs.

Immensely popular the world over, these are like mutual funds which pool resources from small investors and then put the money in real estate projects. These are then listed on the stock market. Like stocks, investors will be able to buy units from both the primary market and the secondary market.

This is a wonderful opportunity for small investors who want to park their savings in real estate but don't know how to go about it. In the absence of REITs, investors need to buy entire flats or plots of land. The ticket size for such investments is large. But there are times when people want to take an exposure to the sector but don't want to commit large chunks of money. This is the perfect investment instrument for such people. Also, this way they can leave the job of risk assessment and management to professional managers.

For real estate projects too, this is a great opportunity. Once REITs become fully functional in the country, a whole range of real estate projects will have easier access to capital.

Of course, more needs to be done.

The Title Act needs to be put in place so that an insurance against land titles is available. There is the need to digitize all land records, which will make transactions transparent and bring down litigation by a third. This will unclog the courts. If you analyse court records, you will find that there are hardly any disputes about share transfers and vehicle sales, but there is a deluge of real estate disputes. Digitization can bring it down to a large extent. Some states like Punjab have taken steps in this direction but a lot more needs to be done in this area.

Is it possible to do business the right way in real estate? Is it possible for a developer to be truthful and ethical? Is it a place for honest and straightforward people at all? The answer, in spite of all the negatives, is that it is possible. If one wants, one can be honest and still be successful in the business.

That's what my experience shows. I am convinced that real estate is no different from any other sector and the same tools of business management apply here. One can use technology, be innovative and build brands in real estate too. Deadlines can be met. Buyers can be happy. Long-term relationships can be built.

Ethics and real estate can go hand in hand.

1

Average Marks

The source of the Yamuna river is the Yamunotri glacier high up in the Himalayas. It is the largest tributary of the Ganges, considered the most sacred river in Hinduism. After merging with other smaller rivers, the Yamuna comes out of the mountains into the plains at Dakpathar near Dehradun. It flows through Paonta Sahib, a pilgrimage spot for Sikhs, and reaches Tajewala in the Yamuna Nagar district of Haryana.

A dam was built here way back in 1873, from which two canals originate: the Eastern Yamuna Canal and the Western Yamuna Canal. The latter irrigates the fields of Haryana and, after being treated at a plant in Haiderpur, its water reaches households in Delhi.

It was at a small village called Dadupur, not far from Tajewala, on the banks of the Western Yamuna Canal, that I was born on 26 October 1963. My family hailed from Kotumber in the Jhelum district, now in Pakistan.

The Jhelum district was famous for providing a large number of soldiers to the British Army before India and Pakistan gained Independence in 1947. The district continues to provide the largest number of personnel to the armed forces in modern-day Pakistan. That's why it is often called the land of martyrs and warriors.

In fact, the town of Jhelum is not very far from the site of the famous battle between Alexander of Macedonia and Porus, the local king.

We were a family of traders. My family was in Kotumber when the Partition violence erupted. In one particularly brutal assault, my grandmother was shot dead by rioters, but my grandfather, Nathu Ram Sayal, survived.

Like most other Hindus and Sikhs who chose to leave Pakistan for India, my grandfather knew there was no future left for his family in the land of his ancestors. He had no option but to give up everything he owned and sought refuge in India.

He moved to Ludhiana, where he bought a shop in the busy Chaura Bazaar and started to re-build his life.

His eldest son, Kharaiti Lal Sayal, was studying law in Kanpur at that time. He was also working part-time to help make both ends meet. Moved by the trauma of Partition and the death of my grandmother, he offered to take care of his siblings: three brothers and a sister.

My family, like hundreds of thousands of other Sikh and Hindu families from Pakistan, had come to India empty-handed. But they refused to be bogged down by their circumstances and, with their trademark indomitable spirit, they were able to rebuild their lives within one generation.

My father, Girdhari Lal Sayal, was born in 1936 and was third among the five siblings. After he passed his class twelve exams in Kanpur, he decided to take up a job as an accounts assistant with the government as he pursued his higher studies.

Persistence paid off. In a few years, he became an accounts officer. He was deputed to the irrigation department of the Punjab government (this is before Haryana was carved out of Punjab in 1966), which brought him to Dadupur.

The story of my mother's family is not very different. They hailed from a place in the Sargodha district near Rawalpindi. Located near Pakistan's capital, Islamabad, Rawalpindi was a big garrison town during the days of the British rule.

Fortunately for the family, my mother's elder brother was in the armed forces. He was able to secure their passage to India. The family hid their gold and other valuables in flour sacks while making their journey across the border. But they were attacked on the way by robbers who threatened to kill all the children unless the family gave them their valuables. They had no choice but to surrender all their jewellery.

They started their journey on foot and continued on horseback until my uncle was able to send army trucks to pick them up and bring them safely to Delhi.

Both families were deeply affected by the Partition, but life had to go on. My elder sister, Poonam, was born in April 1962. I came to this world a year-and-a-half later. My younger sister, Indu, was born ten years after me.

Dadupur was a small irrigation colony. India had been independent for all of fifteen years when my father came to work here. Those were the heady days of a young nation building itself from scratch. Inspired by the success of the Soviet Union, the then prime minister, Jawaharlal Nehru, had drawn up a vision for India where the public sector would act as an engine of growth, and dams and canals were rechristened as the modern-day temples.

There may not have been much in Dadupur by way of infrastructure, but the young government servants like my father were excited to help build the nation and did not mind facing the hardships that came their way.

It was in Dadupur that my education began. There was nothing even remotely fancy about my first school. We all sat on the ground under a large mango tree and listened to our teachers with rapt attention. In the summer, we would come back home with mangoes in our bags and our books in our hands.

All of my primary education happened in Dadupur. The medium of instruction was, of course, Hindi. English was only taught from class five. In fact, till class ten I studied only in Hindi schools in Haryana. So my Hindi was as accented as the natives of the state. When we would come to Delhi to visit friends and relatives, my language was a great source of entertainment for all.

My mother, Shanta, was very strict. In contrast, my father was very lenient with us. He barely raised his voice against us. So we, the kids, would make it a point to enter our home only when my father returned from office in the evening.

Dadupur was in the heart of Haryana. We had buffaloes at home, which gave us sixteen to eighteen litres of milk every day. We had to drink this milk three times a day: morning, evening and night. The slightest refusal would invite my mother's wrath. Yogurt, ghee and other milk products were always available in abundance in the household.

Such a lifestyle, clean and carefree, is unimaginable today. In hindsight, I can say that my mother's anger was only because she would get hassled by our refusal to eat properly. Apart from that, there were no issues between us. Her contribution to our education was substantial. It was difficult for us to bring home a poor mark sheet. These middle-class values, especially the emphasis on education, served my family well.

In recent years, a large number of Indians have made a mark for themselves in the corporate world abroad—Indira Nooyi of PepsiCo, Anshu Jain of Deutsche Bank, Satya Nadella of Microsoft, among others. Time and again, especially in interviews, these successful people have emphasized that education and hard work helped them achieve their success.

Most families knew that good education was the only passport to success in the modern world. Unlike today, there were serious entry barriers if one wanted to enter the world of business; also, businessmen were looked upon with a certain degree of suspicion—a mood so well captured by Satyajit Ray in his 1976 film *Jana Aranya*.

As a result, most people preferred a professional career. Parents made sacrifices to ensure that their children received decent education. In today's knowledge economy, this emphasis on education and hard work has proved to be India's trump card.

It is safe to assume that my mother, having lived through the Partition, knew that her children would not find much success in life unless they were armed with proper education. She may have been a simple housewife, but she was certainly far-sighted when it came to her children's lives.

My father's job was transferable. From Dadupur, he moved to a place called Narwana, and then to Kaithal. It was from Senior Modern School, a private school in Kaithal, that I passed my class ten exams. Randeep Singh Surjewala, the well-known Congress leader in Haryana, was my junior in school.

In school, I excelled in co-curricular activities, especially in oratorical competitions. I would also perform in one-act plays, and recite poetry in Hindi and Sanskrit. At the age of thirteen, I was declared the best speaker in all of Haryana. I won so many awards—at the district as well as state level—that the principal's office ran out of space to stock the cups and trophies!

The awards and accolades, not to forget the frequent cash prizes and the regular mention of my many prizes at the school assembly in the mornings, soon got into my head. I was so involved in co-curricular activities that my studies took a backseat.

The teachers too did not express their displeasure, if they felt any, at my behaviour. I saw no reason to change my ways. As a result, in my class ten exams I scored only 70 per cent marks. Some people may have been satisfied with such a performance, but not my father. He was angry. It was one of the rare occasions when he raised his voice against me. 'Son,' he said, 'if you get such average marks, there is no way you can get into any technical institute. And I don't have enough money to set up a shop for you.'

In today's context, his words may sound strange. After all, there are several options open to youngsters. One can earn a decent living by having excellent oratorical skills alone. There are so many stories of college dropouts setting up billion-dollar businesses, that nobody today loses hope after an 'average' performance in school.

But this was in the 1970s. The original enthusiasm for nation-building had begun to wane. The public sector had begun to run out of steam. The private sector, facing massive obstructions in the form of the Licence Raj and the Quota Raj, had failed to grow beyond a certain size. Growth had fallen to below 3 per cent—it came to be mocked as the Hindu rate of growth.

There were only limited avenues for employment. If one did not become a doctor or an engineer, or failed to secure a government job, one was condemned to a life of ignominy. Educated unemployment had become a serious national threat—in fact, it contributed in no small measure to the 'angry young man' image Amitabh Bachchan made so popular.

There was widespread student unrest in the country over the scarcity of jobs. The most famous of these agitations was led by Jayaprakash Narayan with the call for a 'total revolution'. This was one of the many factors that contributed to Indira Gandhi imposing a national emergency in 1975.

From this perspective, my father's anxiety made perfect sense.

All this while, I had been fascinated by the lives of junior engineers and the overseers in government departments.

I would get to observe them closely wherever my father was posted. They lived in spacious bungalows, moved around in muscular Jeeps, had a small army of servants at home and were always chased by contractors. Their households were always well stocked with goodies. They never seemed short of money.

They were also in high demand in the marriage market. People would give massive dowries to get their daughters married to junior engineers.

I found them fascinating and could not imagine a life better than this. Little did I know that their official income was actually really small and it was bribery that kept their lavish lifestyle going!

I was innocent about the ways of the world. I decided that I too would study hard to become a junior engineer or overseer in a government department.

All of this would sound terribly naïve in today's India. Back then, the country was not just a closed economy but also a closed society. Not only were there very few opportunities for young adults like me, the awareness of the world outside was very low.

Televisions were a luxury. And there was only one broadcaster: the state-owned Doordarshan. Instead of being a window to the rest of the world, it had become a mouthpiece for the government.

The radio was more accessible to the masses, but the situation there was no better. It failed to connect young minds like mine with the rest of the world.

The government, thanks to its socialist leanings, wanted to use it as an agent of social and economic change. The results, at best, were mixed.

In today's world, television has acted as a great equalizer, connecting India to the rest of the world. Mobile phones and the internet have also helped bring different worlds together. People living in slums and shanties now have access to the same information as people living in plush houses and high-rises. This has encouraged people from poor backgrounds to harbour big ambitions. In that sense, the role of television in firing India's entrepreneurial spirit cannot be undermined.

The days of my childhood were different. My dreams were small. Though I had begun to harbour grand dreams— of becoming a junior engineer or overseer—my academic performance failed to improve. My dreams of becoming a civil engineer were dashed when, after class twelve, I failed to secure admission in any engineering college.

In spite of the setback, I was determined to study civil engineering. So, I settled for the second-best option: a diploma course. When I applied to the Haryana Technical Institute, Ambala, I found, much to my horror, that there were no vacancies left in the civil engineering course.

I understood then that, like me, there were many others who dreamt of becoming junior engineers or overseers and living happily ever after. So, I settled for a diploma in mechanical engineering. Back then, there was a provision that if you topped in your section in the first term, you could change your discipline. This was the opening I was looking for. I studied hard, topped my section and promptly applied for a transfer to the civil engineering course. My request was accepted.

My journey as a civil engineer had begun. Little did I realize that this was the first step in my career in the real estate sector.

There was no looking back for me after that. In 1983, when I passed out of Ambala, I had stood second in the whole state. The next task in front of me was to become a junior engineer or overseer.

I soon realized this was easier said than done. Like most junior-level appointments, one needed connections or money to get such a job. One either had to be related to somebody powerful or had to pay a bribe.

I did meet some people who promised me a junior engineer's job, provided I was ready to cough up Rs. 2–3 lakh. It was a large sum of money in the early 1980s. Government servants like my father often retired with amounts much smaller than this in their bank accounts.

Paying these people this much money was firmly ruled out. And we were not related to some powerful leader either, who could get me this job with just a phone call. My dream to become a junior engineer or overseer began to crumble in front of me.

It was then that I got to know that private builders also employed civil engineers in big cities. And each city had its own list of top builders, complete with a proper pecking order. There were no pan-Indian builders back then. That's because real estate had evolved in its own strange way in the country. Land, according to the Constitution, is a state subject. As a result, every state has its own laws for land acquisition and construction. They are always complex and difficult to negotiate, and differ from state to state. You may spend a lifetime understanding the maze of laws in Delhi and will realize that this knowledge will be of no use in neighbouring Gurgaon or Noida.

Also, there was, and continues till date, heavy-duty government intervention at every stage. There was a plethora of clearances and certificates the builder was required to secure from various agencies of the government at every stage of the project. These complexities of the business, not to mention the underhand dealings, drove large corporations away from the real estate sector.

The situation continues to this day: builders from one city have failed to expand into other territories.

At that time, private builders were my only beacon of hope. I began to travel from one construction site in Delhi to another in search of a job, but no opportunities came my way. I was told everywhere that there were vacancies only for people with some work experience.

It was then that an uncle took me to meet Gopal Ansal at his house in the upscale Jorbagh neighbourhood in south Delhi.

Chiranjiv Lal Ansal was a successful Delhi contractor. He wanted his sons—Sushil, Gopal and Deepak—to follow his footsteps and join the family business. But Sushil Ansal, the eldest son, an economics graduate from the prestigious St. Stephen's College, had his own ideas. A better option, he felt, would be to become a builder himself.

Thus, in 1967, he set up Ansal Properties and Infrastructure. In the 1970s, Ansal literally changed the landscape in and around Connaught Place. By the time I completed my diploma, he was the undisputed leader of real estate in Delhi. There were others too like Kailash Nath and Tejwant Singh (or Skipper as we used to call him) but none came close to Ansal. K.P. Singh of DLF, the country's largest and most valuable developer today, was not even in the picture. He was more of a land aggregator than a developer then.

Among builders, Sushil Ansal was the gold standard. While he was the chairman of Ansal Properties and Industries, Gopal Ansal was the managing director.

Sitting in his plush home, Gopal Ansal asked me, 'How much experience do you have?' Of course, I had none. I had been asked this question several times and was at my wit's end. In all naiveté, I replied: 'Sir, please tell me where can I get experience.'

He gave me a hard look.

I think it had occurred to him that if only people with experience were hired, there was no hope ever for a newcomer like me to find a job. He may also have been struck by my innocence. I was immediately offered a job as a trainee engineer at one of his construction sites in Connaught Place. My salary, he said, would be Rs. 690 per month.

2

Screaming in the Corridor

In retrospect, I realize how lucky I was to get a job even before the final results were out. In July, 1983, I reported to work at the construction site of Indra Prakash, 21, Barakhamba Road.

On the first day, because I was the most junior on the technical side, I was assigned the task of counting the trucks that exited the site with excavated earth. A three-level underground basement was being built. And my task was to reconcile the excavated material with the measurement of the pit.

For quite some time I was assigned no other work on the technical side, thanks to the fact I had zero work experience. This wasn't what I had dreamt of doing at all. It was a harsh reality check for a dreamy youngster who had just graduated from college.

With time, strangely, I started enjoying it—not just the mindless counting of trucks but all work, big or small, thrown at me. I took to the whole business like a fish to water.

Life, mind you, was far from comfortable for me. I lived with my parents in Sonepat because my father was posted there. I would catch the daily shuttle service to Delhi at 6.00 a.m. and report for duty at 7.45 a.m. sharp.

On most days, I would be the first at the site. In the evening, I would take the Jhelum Express back and reach home at 10.00 p.m.

One day, the time-keeper who used to deploy the workers according to the day's schedule could not make it to work. The workers were sitting idle. Unless they were assigned their jobs, all work would come to a standstill. Somebody had to make sure that the job was done.

I took the initiative and began assigning the 400 or so workers their tasks. The logjam was broken and the work did not suffer that day.

In a simple way, this shows how motivated employees can make a difference to an organization. Real estate projects often get delayed, thanks to the kind of problem I encountered that day. The builder would have had to pay the workers that day, even if no work had been achieved. Such slip-ups eat into profits.

To restore the profit margins, some builders choose to cut corners. But shabby construction erodes their brand equity, which is bad for business. It is a vicious cycle that has to be nipped in the bud. Organizations need to empower their employees to take initiative on behalf of their colleagues if they fail to show up. Only organizations which institutionalize innovation and risk-taking survive in the long run.

For instance, the Tata Group, which has interests in varied areas as automobile, information technology, steel, chemicals, fertilizers, retail, real estate, tea and coffee, has made a conscious effort to nurture innovative ideas and create the right culture for innovation.

Every year, the group rewards the most innovative ideas that are generated in its various companies. Even ideas that fail are given due recognition. The motivation is to remove the fear of shame and failure from risk-taking. The group does have several innovations to its credit: the small truck Ace in 2005, super-computer Eka in

2005, the Nano car in 2008 and low-cost water purifier Swach in 2012. Unfortunately, such instances are few in India.

Luckily for me, the project head, Mukesh Dham (he later went on to work with DLF and Emaar MGF), had come to the site early and saw me take the initiative. I think his curiosity was aroused. He called me to his office and asked me about my background in detail. His pointed questions soon put me at ease.

'As a civil engineer,' he asked me, 'what is it that you want to achieve in life?' Now that my guard was down, I told him about my dream of a government job with lots of money to spend. 'I don't know when I will get that job,' I concluded. 'I have taken up this job to meet my expenses.' Dham stared at me with his eyes were wide open. 'I appreciate your candour,' he said. 'You want to make money? That you can do through honesty and hard work. I can see that spark in your eyes. You can do it.'

He added that he would tell me stories from his life which would transform my outlook.

The next day, he told his personal assistant to set up a table for me in one corner of his office. Every evening, when the work for the day was done, he would tell me why I shouldn't make money the wrong way.

He gave me examples of people he had worked with. Those who worked dishonestly had to face severe consequences at some point in time or the other. There was a natural justice at play here, some kind of an invisible hand, which punished those who were corrupt and dishonest. The justice would surely come, even if it took time.

Dham also told me that his salary was three times that of any government engineer's, which was an eye-opener for me. Of course, he also knew a lot more than his counterparts from the government.

These conversations indeed began to change me. Very soon, I realized that the only way you can aspire for long-term growth in life is by following the right practices. The job of a junior engineer or overseer began to lose its charm. Dham took me under his wing, and started teaching me the intricacies of construction. It took me very little time to realize that construction in the actual world was totally different from what we had studied in the textbooks.

He pointed out an old Sikh gentleman to me and suggested that I should make him my guru. This man was a senior foreman and had worked on some landmark construction sites in Delhi with a topnotch contractor of that time. A foreman usually leads the workers at a construction site. He reports to the project engineer, and is a buffer between the workers and the management.

Having convinced me to make money the right way in the private sector, Dham clearly wanted me to get acquainted with the most crucial bit of the business: the actual construction.

This is where the builder connected with the buyer. In real estate, reputation is everything. Those who do shoddy construction work find it difficult to get customers.

This became all the more apparent in 2012 and 2013 when it turned from a seller's market to a buyer's market. Those with good brand equity are bound to do better in a slowdown than those who don't care for it. And the best way to control quality is to be aware of the best practices in every field, and masonry is one of them. Masonry is the craft of laying the bricks and spreading the plaster—the two most important jobs in construction.

The foreman, Sardar Jagat Singh, was intelligent but difficult to work with. None of the engineers at the site could match his knowledge in construction. He was aware of it and this had, perhaps, made him contemptuous of engineers in general.

To get into his good books, I began to observe his routine. He had his favourite members of the staff: a mason and two women workers. The four would always work as a team. After the first round of work, Jagat Singh was in the habit of ordering two cups of tea and some snacks, which they would divide amongst themselves.

I decided that I would hang around them during this break. Soon, Jagat Singh was visibly embarrassed to have me standing around while they snacked. After a few days, he asked me to join them for tea. That is how I became a part of their group.

From the next day, I would order tea for all four of them and pay for it. One day, Jagat Singh told me: 'Sahibji, would you like to learn the job?' When I nodded, he smiled and said, 'I will teach you.' He soon became a mentor of sorts for me. Like a helper, I worked with him on setting up benchmarks, levelling, centreing, shuttering and so on.

He was an efficient man. No engineer was capable of doing his work when he chose not to come to the site. But in six months, I was able to do his work on the odd day that he didn't turn up.

Others began to envy me. But Dham was delighted. My interest in the sector had picked up rapidly. I would badger him with questions. For instance, I wanted to know why the owners of the site, the Ansals, never came to see the progress of the project. While Gopal Ansal came once a quarter or so, Sushil Ansal, his older brother and the chairman of the company, would come not more than once a year.

'Do your work. Do not worry about the consequences,' Dham would repeat, sage counsel from the *Gita*.

After a while, Dham began to emphasize the need for a proper engineering degree for me. As a diploma holder, I could grow only up to a certain level. But if I wanted to reach the top, he said I needed a proper degree.

Looking back, I can say that I was lucky to get a superior like Dham so early in my career. Every man, in order to be successful, needs a master who can tell him his shortcomings and show him the right path. In my career, that role was played by Dham. Had it not been for him, I would have wasted a lot of time chasing my fantasies of becoming a junior engineer or overseer in the government.

Heeding Dham's advice, I joined the Institution of Engineers for a civil engineering degree course. I had the option to take the various papers over two years, but Dham insisted I take them all in the first year itself. I decided to write all the tests in one go.

One had to obtain either 200 marks in aggregate or had to score 50 per cent in each subject to pass. When the marks were aggregated, I had scored 199. But luck intervened. The Institution of Engineers that year came out with an offer that if a candidate had appeared in all the papers and his marks were just one short of the required aggregate of 200, he would still be awarded the degree. I was the first beneficiary. The milestone had been achieved.

A whole lot of my friends, who were now working for different companies, had also taken the exams with me. The day the results were declared, my friends came to the site and asked me to accompany them to check the results.

There was no internet at that time. The results were displayed on a notice board at the Institution of Engineers near Bahadur Shah Zafar Marg. Since there was some important casting work going on at the site, I expressed my inability to go and asked them to inform me later. They asked for my roll number. The number I told them wasn't the right one, though it was quite similar to it.

A little while later, they came back to say that none of us had made it, though a number similar to mine was on the list. Before parting, they offered to take me out in the evening so we could all drown our sorrows in a drink or two.

By now, my heart was pounding. I quickly wrapped my work up and made a dash for the Institution of Engineers. My prayers were answered. I indeed was the lucky one. It was one of the happiest moments of my life.

I joined my friends in the evening and broke the news to them. The party was on me. I then took the last train to Sonepat at 10.30 p.m. I was very keen to break the news to my mother.

She used to stay awake till late at night while I was studying for the exams. A few days before the results were announced, she had become very anxious about my welfare. Perhaps out of sheer exhilaration, I fell asleep as soon as I boarded the train. I woke up with a start and asked the other passengers how close we were to Sonepat. They gave me incredulous looks. 'We crossed it an hour ago,' one of them said.

In fact, the train had just started rolling out of the Ganaur railway station when I woke up. I lunged for the exit. It was biting cold outside and I couldn't see a soul on the platform. Yet, I jumped out of the train.

As I moved out of the station, I found a bunch of ragpickers. When I asked them if I could find a place in the town to spend the night, they pointed to a Jain dharamshala. I made my way there and knocked on its doors. But nobody came out.

While the keeper of the dharamshala did not respond, a man from a nearby house woke up and came to ask me what happened. I told him the whole story. He said that I could spend the night at his house and catch the early-morning train to Sonepat. He then laid out a bed for me and gave me blankets to keep me warm. His wife even gave me a glass of hot milk. Next morning, at 4.30 a.m., she woke me up with a cup of steaming hot tea—just in time for me to catch the morning train. That episode left a lasting imprint on my mind. Two strangers came out of nowhere to help me.

I am convinced that god, in his infinite wisdom, created the whole situation to drive home the importance of being a good human being. While it is good to be successful in life, it is more important to be kind towards others.

At 6.00 a.m., I was home. Mother was at the door, waiting for me. There were tears in her eyes. She had obviously not slept the whole night, waiting for me to return from Delhi. There were no mobile phones at that time, so there was no way I could have informed her that I was safe. While I tried telling her my experience, she brushed it all aside. 'You are an adult now,' she said. 'You don't need me anymore.'

Then I produced the tin of rasagullas that I had purchased for her. But she brushed it aside. 'Don't try to bribe me.' She was tough and tolerated no nonsense from her kids, but she was also very kind. When I broke the news that her son was now a full-fledged engineer, she couldn't control her emotions. Tears of joy spilled out of her eyes.

Clearing the exams in a single shot instilled a great deal of self-assurance in me. My spirits were soaring and my confidence was rising. I knew I could do even better in life. Nothing, after all, succeeds like success.

There would be no stopping me after that. Promotions began to come thick and fast at work.

In 1988, I got a job offer from another builder. An acquaintance, who was the chief engineer with this builder, took me to meet him. He lived in great style in a spacious bungalow. In his offer to me, he threw in a Maruti 800. This little car had revolutionized India. It was the dream of every middle-class Indian to own this dainty little car, which was easy to maintain and highly fuel-efficient. I took up the offer.

Within two years of working for him, the excitement quickly turned to shock. Under his wing, I learnt how not to do business. His business mantra was: as long as there are fools out there, our business will carry on.

The builder was thoroughly unscrupulous, to say the least. He would sell the same commercial property to four, or even five, buyers.

Once, an old man had come to meet him in his office with a bagful of money. As long as he had not handed over the money, the builder was extremely courteous to him. But his demeanour began to change when the money changed hands. Five minutes after leaving the office, the old man came back for one final word with the builder—and he was refused a meeting! Uttering a thick expletive, the builder asked his secretary to get some junior employee to meet the man. I was shocked at this blatant display of indecency.

Worse was to come. The builder had launched apartments in Delhi's suburbs at unbelievably low prices. Everybody was wondering how he would be able to construct houses with such low price tags. But the buyers suspected nothing wrong. Poor people lined up in front of his office, their hard earned money tied in bundles and placed carefully inside grimy plastic bags, to book these flats.

Obviously, the builder never really planned to construct those houses. His sole objective was to dupe poor people. He knew they wouldn't be able to hire expensive lawyers or pull some strings to recover their money. He exploited their situation thoroughly. Indeed, a lot of people lost their money in that housing project.

Soon there came a time when there would be two queues in front of his office: one that wanted to book flats and the other that wanted its money back. It still saddens me to think about what this builder did to so many poor people. The long arm of law did catch up with him eventually.

If the builder was horrible to his customers, he was no better with his employees. They didn't get their salaries on time. Since most of them made money on the sly—the rot ran so deep in the organization—nobody complained. Everybody seemed to be happy with the state of affairs.

However, I told him that since I did not make money like that, I ought to get my salary on time. The builder instructed his secretary that my salary should be disbursed on the first day of every month 'or else, this person will shout and scream in the corridor'.

I have often wondered how a totally amoral builder like him could survive in the market for so long. How did he manage to con so many people? The only answer I have is that awareness was very low at that time.

As it is, real estate was and remains an opaque sector. On the other hand, the builder never faced any problem while seeking clearances from the government because he was superbly connected. His parties boasted of all the movers and shakers in the capital at that time. Anybody who mattered would make it a point to attend the parties at his spacious house. And it was at his parties that I developed a taste for good Scotch whisky.

In January 1988, I got married. In November the same year, my wife, Kanika, and I were blessed with a baby girl, Aayushi.

In 1990, I was contacted by the Ansals. Life had come a full circle: while seven years ago, I had approached them for a job, this time they came to me. They were putting up another residential project around Connaught Place: Dhawan Deep at 6, Jantar Mantar Road. The owners of this plot of land were related to Sushil Ansal. The Ansals wanted me to become the project manager.

This was an enormous display of faith in me. In the Ansal group, one became a project manager only after fifteen years of experience. I had seven. There was some resistance from within the group, but Gopal Ansal insisted the job should be given to me.

This was also a good way for me to break all ties with the unscrupulous builder. I had been on his rolls for almost two years now. His reputation was on the brink of collapse. Had I stayed on a little longer, my job prospects too would have diminished. I took up the Ansal offer. This was my seventh promotion in as many years.

As the project manager, I was in charge of the construction. I was responsible not only for executing the project according to the design finalized but also handing it over within the deadline. I would have to interact with the architects and the contractors, as well as the buyers sent to the site by the sales office. The project was worth Rs. 15–20 crore—not a small amount of money in those days.

Fate intervened again after I had completed almost 85 per cent of the project.

3

Working with Pickles

It could be a story straight out of a Bollywood flick. Kushal Pal Singh studied at a madrasa, became part of the British high society in England and then joined the Indian Army. But he soon resigned his commission because he had to help his father-in-law, Chaudhary Raghvendra Singh, in business.

After trying his hand at other industries (Willard and American Universal), K.P. Singh took it upon himself to revive the fortunes of his father-in-law's almost defunct company, Delhi Land & Finance (DLF) Ltd. Though DLF had built some colonies in Delhi in the 1960s, the government had subsequently decided to take all urban development in its own hands. So DLF was left with no business, and Chaudhary Raghvendra Singh had decided to sell it for Rs. 27 lakh.

Singh felt that the business could see a turnaround in its fortunes and pleaded with his father-in-law for a chance to run the company.

His father-in-law probably had little to lose and handed the company over to his son-in-law. Over the next few years, the company chugged along. It did nothing spectacular, but it didn't fold either.

Singh says in his biography that the turning point in his life came in the 1980s. One hot day, while he was sitting on a charpoy under a tree in Gurgaon, a car screeched to a halt and the driver asked for water to cool the engine. The driver was Rajiv Gandhi, the future prime minister of India and son of the then prime minister Indira Gandhi. In his book, *Against All Odds*, Singh recounts how that fateful day he sold Rajiv the dream of suburban development. And that is how Gurgaon came up.

At that time, Delhi was bursting at its seams. There weren't enough homes to accommodate the thousands who were migrating to the city from across the country every day. Singh cleverly positioned his residential development in Gurgaon as 'south Delhi' by naming it Qutub Enclave.

After that, there was no looking back for the man and his company, DLF. It is India's most valuable real estate company today and Singh is amongst the richest men of India. Various lists of the country's richest people always feature him. In recent years, the DLF share price has shed value, which has affected Singh's net worth, but it is still substantial.

He owns more than one house in the Lutyens Zone of New Delhi, perhaps the most expensive patch of land in the country. It is not for nothing that Singh's DLF is often expanded to stand for 'Damn Lucky Fellow'.

When I was working my second stint with the Ansals, I had a couple of friends who worked with DLF—R.K. Verma and Rajiv Malhotra. They were deputed to work on DLF Centre, which was coming up in Connaught Place.

Back then, Connaught Place was Delhi's prime business district and housed all the top companies: Maruti Suzuki, Escorts and Ranbaxy. You weren't a builder of repute if you didn't have a signature building here. DLF Centre was the company's centrepiece in the area.

We used to compare notes often and share technical knowhow. I came to know from them that Gurgaon was slowly shaping up to become a most sought after residential hub. DLF was building Beverley Park I and II—both bustling upscale neighbourhoods today. They wanted me to join the company as the project head of Beverley Park I.

This was in 1993. The economy was on the upswing. Changing jobs quickly had become the norm. Old-fashioned loyalty of working for a company your entire life had gone out of fashion.

DLF too was morphing into a new-age builder. Rajiv Singh, K.P. Singh's son, was now involved in the business and he wanted to bring about a paradigm shift in the way the company functioned. He talked of high-tech equipment and had a grand vision for the growth of DLF. He also wanted to do everything in-house: design, architecture and construction. He bought all the equipment that was required for it.

Today, the management debate over doing everything in-house versus outsourcing is more or less settled. The current wisdom is that a company needs to stick to its core competence and outsource all other work. Large telecom service operators, for instance, hand over all network management services to vendors. Similarly, companies in the durables space outsource consumer interface to professionals. Business corporations across the world hire contractors to run and maintain their information technology backbone. Some even outsource key functions like accounts and payroll.

At that time, this view hadn't evolved. Many businessmen thought it was best to have integrated operations so that they could keep a close watch on quality and protect their margins (Henry Ford even wanted to set up a huge plantation in Brazil, which would provide all the rubber needed for the tyres his company produced).

Rajiv Singh too believed that by doing everything in-house, it would help the company maintain standards. DLF had even diversified into cement as backward integration. It subsequently sold the business to Gujarat Ambuja (now known as Ambuja Cements). Many people were quick to jump ship and join DLF. But I had my reservations. Rajiv Singh was the sole coordinator in-charge of the company's transformation; but when you spoke to others in the organization they didn't have a clue about what was happening.

Change has to be institutionalized if you want it to last. It cannot simply be driven down from the top. Everybody has to be taken on board. The vision—and the route to that vision—needs to be articulated to all employees. Only then can the whole process of change occur organically.

A company, for that matter any organization, is made up of people who come together with a common vision. If that vision has to change, everybody needs to be convinced. They should buy into this need for change 100 per cent. Nobody can be left out. Success cannot be built on the backs of disgruntled or indifferent employees. Otherwise, the whole purpose of the exercise is defeated.

That is why an effective leader has to, first and foremost, be an effective communicator. This has been the hallmark of global corporate leaders like Jack Welch, Steve Jobs and Bill Gates. Closer home, doyens of the industry, leaders like Ratan Tata, Azim Premji and N.R. Narayana Murthy owe their success to the fact that they communicated their vision very well to all the stakeholders, including employees and customers.

Communication is more than just playing the media game. Some use it to drum up their share price, settle scores with a rival, send out signals to prospective business partners or drive sales. A good communicator also addresses the concerns and anxieties of all stakeholders, and answers all their questions patiently.

In DLF's case, I felt the vision was good but the hierarchy had not bought Rajiv Singh's vision 100 per cent. This was bound to cause some discordance and friction. I felt uncomfortable.

All of this was playing on my mind. I knew there was not much space for an upswing in my career graph with Ansal. If I continued working there, there was no way I would be able to broaden my mental and professional horizons. But I was wary that I might take an unwise decision in haste.

The golden rule is always consider a career switch when you think you have reached the peak at your current job. Otherwise, there is a good chance of the decision going horribly wrong.

For a couple of months, I debated the offer from DLF in my head. I wasn't enjoying my job and here was this opportunity to work with one of the fastest-growing real estate companies. I knew the long-term prospects were good: It had enough land bank to last for another twenty to thirty years.

But fate had something else in store for me. Destiny often works in the most mysterious ways. One day, in the *Times of India*, I saw an advertisement placed by a private sector shipping company that was looking for real estate professionals in north India. There were no other details available.

I didn't have the faintest clue about who had placed the advertisement. Nevertheless, I was interested. Over the next few days, I put together my biodata—for the first time in my life—and sent it to the address mentioned in the newspaper.

I knew I was groping in the dark but I decided to risk it. After all, I had nothing to lose. Only when the reply to my application came that I learnt that the company was, in fact, the Great Eastern Shipping Company.

The Great Eastern Shipping Company was started by the Sheth (Mulji) and Bhiwandiwalla families who wanted to expand the footprint of their trading business. Brothers Maneklal Ujmashi Mulji and Jagjivan Ujmashi Mulji were textile traders who subsequently entered the sugar business. They made it so big in the trade of this commodity that Maneklal came to be called 'Sugar King', while Jagjivan was called 'Sugar Bapa'.

Their partner was Ardeshir Hormusji Bhiwandiwalla, a Parsi gentleman. They had some idea of how the shipping business worked thanks to their sugar trade, and they decided to enter the sector.

The Great Eastern Shipping Company started operations in 1948 when the SS *Fort Elice*, a mothballed ship it had acquired, set sail. The business was run by Vasant J. Sheth, Jagjivan's son.

Under his stewardship, the company grew from strength to strength. When I was called for an interview in the early months of 1993, the Great Eastern Shipping Company was the country's largest such organization in the private sector and was sitting on a cash pile of Rs. 1,000 crore.

These days when start-ups are raising capital worth hundreds of millions of dollars in less than a year, it might seem like very little money. At that time, however, it was huge. Most companies could only dream of having so much cash in their kitty. Now, the Great Eastern Shipping Company was looking for places to invest this money.

Real estate was the chosen avenue. I was never told why this unrelated diversification was planned. It is safe to assume that the company was looking at emerging sectors, and real estate, with the demand falling way short of the supply available, looked like a safe bet.

I was called for an interview at the Great Eastern Shipping Company liaison office at 3, Rajdoot Marg, in New Delhi's diplomatic enclave. The human resources team had come down from Mumbai.

There, I met Col. R.S. 'Pickles' Sodhi who was all set to join the real estate venture. It was the beginning of a long association.

Col. Sodhi was a cavalry officer and had taught horse riding to Sudhir Mulji, the vice-chairman of Great Eastern Shipping Company (Mulji was also an economist and an accomplished newspaper columnist; he died in England in July 2005). They were very close to one another.

According to one account, Nafisa Ali, the actress and champion swimmer, stayed at Mulji and his wife Rosaleen's house after she married Col. Sodhi. During one of their meetings, Col. Sodhi had told Mulji that he was frustrated with the Army and was looking for a change.

Mulji asked him to join the real estate venture his company was floating. He knew that Col. Sodhi would not have much experience in this sector but his long innings in the armed forces had taught him excellent human resources management skills. Col. Sodhi agreed to Mujli's offer. At the time of my interview, he was not fully on board. Still, he was on the interview panel.

The interview progressed well. At the end of it, they offered me the post of deputy manager. I refused because I didn't see it as an elevation in my status—I wasn't even being made a full-fledged manager.

After the interview, Col. Sodhi took me aside and said that he had joined as manager, and if the designation of deputy manager was not to my liking, he would step aside so that I could become the manager. He also explained that in this company, the manager's rank was equivalent to that of a general manager in other companies. So, as deputy manager, I would fall in the same grade as a deputy general manager in other companies.

I was touched by his gesture. How many people are capable of showing so much magnanimity to a total stranger? It also made me feel good about myself: my superior was ready to make personal sacrifices to get me on board.

Accepting this offer meant saying no to DLF, which was a significantly bigger name in this part of the country, but I decided to go ahead with my gut feeling.

The Great Eastern Shipping Company was among the few business conglomerates that were trying their hand at real estate. At that time, some large companies like Videocon and Mahindra & Mahindra had tried to leverage their land bank to get into the sector, but only in a limited way.

That's because the business was highly unregulated and hence, open to manipulation. Too much power in the hands of bureaucrats and ministers has always bred corruption. Since they all stand to lose in a big way if the processes are simplified, they offer maximum resistance to any proposed change. It is a well-oiled system in which everybody, from the top to the bottom, gets a cut. There is a lot of incentive for the lawmakers and bureaucrats to let this corruption persist.

At that time, in Delhi, it was possible for one to have a turnover of Rs. 110 crore in real estate with just Rs. 10 crore in your pocket.

Real estate worked a lot like forward trading. People used to go to a government auction by pooling together investments from ten people. This would help them make the first payment to the Delhi Development Authority (DDA). Then, without getting the title, without any approval, the builder used to sell the project and collect the money. So the developer never actually invested his own money in the acquisition of the property.

There was minimal risk and maximum return in the sector. This way, the builder was able to invest in several projects simultaneously.

Inordinate delays were the norm. If you take the example of the downtown area of Connaught Place, none of the projects were completed in less than seven or eight years; some even took nine or ten years to finish.

Getting all the clearances could take two to four years and would cost a lot of money. The builders would recover these costs by constructing more than what was authorized. This is where they made real money.

Basements meant for parking were converted into offices. Security guidelines were grossly neglected. The buildings were of very poor quality, the builders used the worst possible construction material. The results can be seen at Nehru Place and Rajendra Place, which have often been described as the 'corporate slums of New Delhi'.

Most of these properties didn't even possess a proper completion certificate. Still, thanks to rampant corruption, they were given electricity connections and the builders were able to sell space.

The hapless buyer didn't have even the faintest idea that the space sold to him was illegal. Many would manage to get their constructions 'regularized'. In fact, this has been the bane of urban planning in Delhi. For electoral gains, the state government frequently 'regularizes' unauthorized colonies. Since builders know their illegal constructions can be made legitimate by paying a bribe, they flout every rule in the book right from day one.

The rot in the system was exposed by the Uphaar tragedy.

On Friday, 13 June 1997, a fire broke out at Uphaar Cinema, located in the Green Park area of south Delhi, during a matinee (3 p.m. to 6 p.m.) show of *Border*. Fifty-nine people died, mostly of suffocation, and 103 were injured in the stampede that ensued.

The fire started at the transformer located at the basement of the hall. There were thirty-six cars parked there, against the permitted eighteen, of which twenty were gutted in the fire. The transformer was maintained by the Delhi Vidyut Board, a government agency.

During the investigations that followed, it became clear that every malpractice had been followed while building the hall. The gangways were blocked as the cinema hall had taken up the space to accommodate more seats. Empty spaces, which would have come handy in such a situation, had been converted into shops. The fire exits were locked.

A magisterial inquiry, which submitted its report on 3 July 1997, held the cinema management, Delhi Vidyut Board, the city fire service, the Delhi police's licensing branch and the Municipal Corporation responsible for the incident saying 'it contributed to the mishap through acts of omission and commission'.

The Ansals, who owned Ansals Club Hotels and Theatres, which ran the cinema hall, were later taken into judicial custody.

Everyone in the real estate sector was horrified by the event. It was a case of gross negligence on the part of the authorities too. While the liabilities of the directors of the company were clearly listed in the Companies Act, there was nothing stated anywhere to pull up erring bureaucrats who glossed over the violations and allowed the cinema hall to run. It is this murkiness that had kept large corporations away from Delhi's real estate market.

Still, the Great Eastern Shipping Company, which had a strong reputation for being an ethical company, felt there was scope to do business the right way without bending the rules, and therefore, decided to enter the business.

Initially, real estate was just a division in the company, but later, it had to be demerged into a separate company called Gesco Corporation in 1999.

The Great Eastern Shipping Company had done some real estate projects in Mumbai and now wanted to enter the market in New Delhi. When I joined, there was one administrative officer and a peon.

We operated out of the Rajdoot Marg liaison office. There were two or three bedrooms there, meant for visitors from Mumbai. We were asked to operate out of one of those. And when that room was booked for a visitor, the three of us would move into the reception area and work from there.

Of course, there was no project in hand, which meant there was absolutely no work to do. Frustration began to set in. But all of that was going to change soon.

The Great Eastern Shipping Company had this culture of calling senior managers and business heads to Mumbai for review meetings. One day, it was my turn to go there. At the meeting, I came face-to-face with Ghanshyam Sheth for the first time.

He was looking after the real estate business in Mumbai. He asked me how I planned to establish the company's presence in Delhi. I gave him my objective view of the business reality. This is a sector, I told him, that is not organized at all, promises are seldom kept and things roll on the wheels of money. I listed out the rules of the game matter-of-factly.

Before I could proceed any further, Sheth signalled me to come out of the room. Without raising his voice, without any trace of anger, he said, 'Mr. Sayal, do not use these words ever again. We know about it but this is not the way we do business. If speed money is required, we don't get into that venture at all.'

His words were an eye-opener. Till that moment, it hadn't occurred to me that the real estate business could be conducted with absolute honesty and ethics. In my limited worldview, palms had to be greased and corners had to cut to ensure the project was completed.

I had not indulged in any corrupt practices myself because I was just a project manager and it was not my job to chase bureaucrats, senior or junior, for the various clearances. I had based my observations on everything I had seen that far and what

I had gathered while talking to my seniors. I was not off the mark. Sheth knew that, but he had decided that he would have none of it.

At that time, this focus on ethics was indeed praiseworthy. Till 1991, two years before I joined the Great Eastern Shipping Company, we had the Licence Raj, which vested absolute power in the hands of the political class and the bureaucrats. Corruption and business were inseparable. For somebody to eschew such practices altogether showed a mindset that was well ahead of its time.

Now, of course, there is a wide body of research which shows that ethical companies which maintain the highest standards of transparency and corporate governance are rewarded better in the stock market.

Watchdogs in the form of investor advisors are on the prowl these days, on the lookout for the slightest violation of corporate governance norms. One adverse report can destroy the trust of the shareholders. At least three such watchdogs are active in India: InGovern, Stakeholders' Empowerment Services and Institutional Investors Advisory Service. In the last few years, they have pulled up venerated names like TVS Motor Company, Hindalco, Jindal Steel & Power and Infosys.

They go through corporate announcements, analyse them and then take a view on it. In the soul searching done by regulators after the massive Satyam scam came to light, one of the issues that came up was the apathy towards voting activity by institutional shareholders, which typically hold considerable stakes in large companies. Many mutual funds never voted.

Then, the Securities and Exchange Board of India, or SEBI, said in March 2010 that all institutions would have to disclose how they vote on various resolutions. Funds and institutions had hundreds of companies in their portfolio. Their grouse was that if they started analysing every resolution and took a voting decision on these, they would be left with little time for managing money.

This triggered the birth of proxy advisory firms. All this has to some extent helped the cause of corporate governance. In the early 1990s, such checks and balances did not exist. Bending the rules and paying bribes were accepted business practices—at least in the real estate sector. Not for nothing, businessmen in popular culture of the time—films and literature—were always portrayed as corrupt, cunning and unscrupulous. It is only in recent years that their image has seen some improvement.

Was I offended by what Sheth said? Not in the least. I felt as if somebody had shaken me out of deep slumber and opened my eyes. I did not feel slighted by Sheth's words. In fact, it had the reverse impact on me. It filled me with immense energy.

Back in New Delhi the next morning, I called all the brokers I knew and explained to them how we proposed to do business. My enthusiasm clearly didn't have any impact on them. 'You have joined a good company, but, with this attitude, it won't last six months in the market,' one of them said. 'Enjoy your salary till then, Mr. Sayal.'

The unanimous view was that by choosing the moral high-ground, it would be impossible for us to get any business or bag any project. But that did not deter me.

I had told all brokers that if they had a large land parcel, we would be interested in buying it. We scouted for land in south Delhi. Every day I would meet at least two or three brokers. I was shown some big properties, but almost all of them had some title hassle or the other. In some cases, the owners demanded cash. This was unacceptable to us. We were not prepared to make even the tiniest compromise.

It soon began to appear as if I had reached a dead-end. Then, one day I came across an advertisement by the Delhi

Development Authority that it would auction land at Bhikaji Cama Place, a commercial area in south Delhi named after the famous Zoroastrian freedom fighter.

The address was 2A, Bhikaji Cama Place. It was a small plot of land sandwiched between the offices of two state-owned enterprises: Engineers India and Punjab National Bank. In an earlier auction, Kailash Nath & Associates, another leading Delhi builder, had got the land but the Delhi Development Authority had taken it back for some reason.

Because of this, many people were not interested in the auction. They feared there could be legal hassles over the title deed.

For us, this was the opening we were looking for. We flew down to Mumbai and told our superiors that this was our opportunity. The titles were all clean. Approvals wouldn't pose a problem since it was a Delhi Development Authority auction. There was no question of bribing the bureaucrats. And no under-the-table money was required to be taken from the buyers.

The sales pitch worked. The board asked us to go ahead and bid for the project. Even if we do not make any money, we were told, we should go for it. It would help us establish ourselves in Delhi.

We had about sixty days to go before the auction. This gave us some time to take care of the documentation and prepare our bid. Sheth asked us to prepare a feasibility report for the project. He repeatedly emphasized on balancing the corporation's need to generate profit vis-à-vis its duty to 'leave something on the table for the buyer(s)'.

This was easier said than done: We had never prepared such a report before. I spoke to some professionals, including architects and lawyers, for advice.

In those days, this work wasn't too evolved. People often prepared these reports by comparing the values of similar projects and in fact, many of them wrote their reports based on their gut instinct. It is only in recent years that the whole process has become more scientific. Current valuations are arrived at by discounting future earnings. At that time, one went by guesstimates.

Still, we were able to put together a report. One of the people who helped us prepare the pre-bid documents was S.C. Nanda, the prominent real estate lawyer. It was a great learning experience for all of us. Confident that we had a proper report, I took it to Mumbai so our bosses could vet it.

Our efforts hadn't been in vain. The bosses liked the report and gave us their go-ahead. Then and there we made a plan for the bidding. Bubbling with energy, I came back and we started preparing for the big day.

Although the company had sanctioned a bid of up to Rs. 11 crore, we won the auction at Rs. 8.78 crore in May 1993. Other builders like the Ansals, Som Dutt and Kailash Nath too had participated in the process but we were able to outbid all of them. The plot of land was ours.

After we acquired the title for the land, I travelled to Mumbai again to meet the bosses. It was decided that we would keep all our promises and honour our commitments.

We had audaciously promised that we would finish the project in fourteen months flat, once all the approvals were obtained.

There is a lot of literature available on how to set targets. Most companies go through historical as well as comparative data to do that. If one were to look at such data, our target was truly ambitious.

When we showed our business plan to the brokers, they all unanimously agreed that we had lost our minds—nobody can deliver a project of this size in such little time. We were told that even if we constructed the building at the fastest speed the market had ever seen, it would take us at least four years.

It was a tough challenge, but we decided to take it up. It would have been easy for us to drag the construction on for three or four years—nobody would have complained because that was the norm. But we had to make a statement in the market.

At that time, commercial real estate was like a commodity; all builders were alike. They all delayed projects, overbuilt and, thanks to all the corruption around, cut corners unscrupulously. We wanted to be different. We decided to not just finish the project well in time, but to ensure that every rule and guideline was followed.

This was also the time the Indian economy was opening up. Foreign companies were setting up offices in the country. India was an untapped market of a billion people. All of a sudden, every multinational corporation was keen to expand in the country. Many saw it as the final frontier of business.

Indian skills in information technology had come to be recognized as the best in the world. Jack Welch of GE, a personal friend of K.P. Singh, had spotted potential in locating call centres in India.

This was going to raise the demand for quality real estate. As a result, more discerning buyers were coming to the market. They were ready to pay a premium for the right office space— one that was efficient, well-managed and, most importantly, free of irregularities. Nobody wanted to squander their managerial bandwidth by grappling with real estate snags.

We had set up a stiff completion deadline and, therefore, had a real challenge on our hands. I set up my project office in a portable cabin next to the construction site. Later, we shifted it to

Col. Sodhi's house in Greater Kailash: it was in the lobby in front of the kitchen.

My first task was to appoint an architect for the project. Fortunately, we had met several of them while preparing the bid document and we shortlisted four architects. Accompanied by Sudhir Mulji, we decided to visit each of them in their offices.

After much thought and discussion, we decided to go with Rajendra Kumar. He was considered amongst the best architects in Delhi and had worked on many prestigious buildings in the city.

The presentation he made at his office in Safdarjung Enclave was outstanding and, more importantly, we really liked the man. We gave him a brief idea of what we had in mind. We decided to call the building 'Great Eastern Plaza'.

Kumar said he would charge us 4 per cent of the development cost (except land) as his fees. Most architects at that time charged 5 per cent but that was open to negotiation. Almost every architect used to lament that their payments were invariably delayed because of the several setbacks in the projects. Their frustration with the builders ran high.

We were not keen on negotiating the fees because we wanted high-quality work, timely service and full accountability. When we told the architects that we wanted to finish the project in just fourteen months, they said it was difficult but not impossible. That was comforting.

The final piece of the jigsaw was the construction. We said we would hire the best contractor in the business. Through our architects, we decided to call for bids. Normally, the practice is to hand out the contract to the lowest bidder. We decided not to go by financial parameters but to look at the track record and the reputation of the contractors.

Finally, we chose Tirathram Ahuja & Associates. It was a firm of high repute and had constructed the iconic Ashok Hotel and several embassies in the city. And it had quoted the highest amount.

In hindsight, this was the perfect entry strategy for the company. We had a clean property, we promised speedy completion and we had hired the best architect and construction contractor in town. Of course, we could have saved some money by hiring some other architect or contractor, but our reputation would have taken a hit.

Delays and substandard construction would have bracketed us with all the other builders of the town. We didn't want that to happen. What we had promised was nothing short of a paradigm shift in the way we negotiated the real estate market.

While the practice of hiring the lowest bidder may work in government contracts where public money is involved, it need not always be the best policy for private corporations.

We had to build our reputation, our brand. And that takes some effort. At times, one has to forgo profits—at least in the short run—in order to establish one's reputation and brand.

In real estate, reputation matters more than anything else. And we wanted to build our reputation for producing high-quality work by following clean business practices. This strategy helped us enter the market at the top of the value chain. If you enter at the bottom, it is almost impossible to move up to the top. Like in personal matters, in business too, the first impression is often the last.

Sardar Prithpal Singh, the co-owner of the construction firm, was touched by our gesture. He took it up as a personal challenge to complete the project on time. Instead of appointing a professional, he began to supervise the work himself. He would come to the site almost every day and work as if he was the project manager.

And the miracle happened. We completed the Great Eastern Plaza and got the completion certificate within fourteen months. It was fully in compliance with all the laws and bylaws. There wasn't a single violation. This had never happened in Delhi before.

The building was ready to be sold.

4

Breaking Out

We did not want to lease out the Bhikaji Cama Place building. Our plan was to sell it off. And unlike the other buildings in the area, we didn't wish to sell it to a large number of buyers. This would have turned the Great Eastern Plaza into a substandard address.

This is precisely what happened to the commercial district of Nehru Place in south Delhi. Several companies had bought space there in the 1970s and 1980s. Once they grew in size, the organizations found it hard to expand their offices because each building was parcelled into smaller pieces and sold to a large number of buyers. It became an urban commercial slum. In a matter of years, most of these companies moved out of Nehru Place. Moreover, because there were a large number of tenants, the maintenance of these buildings was never done properly.

The same problem afflicted Bhikaji Cama Place. And we wanted to avoid it. After constructing a top-class building in record time, we didn't want it to look shabby. Otherwise, the image we wanted to build would have taken a serious beating— nothing can be more disastrous for a company looking to enter a new market.

So we decided to sell entire floors of the building, as opposed to individual offices. We knew it would take more time to sell, but we were out to create a brand. The ticket size was large and there were few takers for that much space.

Still, by the time the construction was completed, we had managed to sell two floors: one to Living Media (the publishers of *India Today*) and the other to Punj Lloyd (a construction and engineering company). But there was no other buyer. Still, we were convinced that we had a good thing going and were determined that, come what may, we would not undersell it.

Meanwhile, we had started to scout for more projects. What next after Great Eastern Plaza? The question had started to bother us. Somebody told us of a property—an empty patch of land roughly an acre in size—on the now stylish Mehrauli–Gurgaon Road.

However, the land was on the wrong side of the road— towards old Gurgaon, the unglamourous part of the city. But I felt that given enough time, this area would also develop and there would be buyers for this property.

I met the owner of the property and he said he would accept payment only in cash. This was a problem as we didn't deal in cash. I asked him why he needed such a payment. He was a practical man. He said he would buy some other commercial property, which would require liquid cash, and earn a regular rental income from it.

I offered him a solution. Let's get into a barter agreement, I told him, where you give us your land and, in return, we will give you half a floor at the Great Eastern Plaza. He would get a regular income by leasing out that space, and we could stick to our principle of not dealing in cash.

At that time, Ericsson, the telecom company, was looking for office space in the city. The Delhi Development Authority had come down heavily on companies operating out of residential areas and shops, and had sealed the Ericsson office in Hauz Khas.

The company was looking for 50,000 to 60,000 square feet of office space. In Delhi, at that time, there was no building which could offer so much space. The matter was presented to us. We had the space as our floor area was 70,000 square feet, but Ericsson was keen to take it on lease and was reluctant to buy it.

We took the proposal to our board, who had asked us to sell the building and not lease any of the space. The board heard out my solution, but remained adamant about selling space in the building.

It would have been blunt on my part to tell Ericsson that its offer was unacceptable—in business, it is unwise to break off ties abruptly. To put off the company, we quoted a monthly rent of Rs. 175 per square foot—four times the prevailing rate of Rs. 40 to 45 per square foot. And Ericsson agreed!

I called up Sheth in Mumbai. His resistance crumbled. He asked us to conclude the agreement as soon as possible. We leased out all the floors—including the ones sold to Living Media, Punj Lloyd and Bindal—to Ericsson, except the one floor which was taken by British Aerospace.

At the end, the project had cost us around Rs. 25 crore. And it was fetching us monthly rent of Rs. 1.2 crore—that's an annual income of over Rs. 14 crore. The return on investment was not a small amount. Had the Great Eastern Shipping Company invested this money in any other avenue—bullion, stock market, fixed deposit or any other business—there was no way it could have generated such handsome returns.

Naturally, this whetted the company's appetite. It wanted us to take up more projects and replicate the success story of the Great Eastern Plaza.

This was also the time I started to build my team. The idea was to have a team of young professionals with the fires of ambition still burning in them. It is an open secret that with age, the appetite to take risks comes down. That's why people who are older like to play it safe.

This may be alright for an organization that is well established, but would certainly not do for one like ours. We were raring to go and, therefore, could not afford to have on board people who didn't want to take risks.

The first person I took on was Mukul Kumar who had worked with me earlier. He was put in charge of construction. Pradipta Sen joined us to take care of the business centre activities.

For finance, the Great Eastern Shipping Company office in Mumbai had referred a young chartered accountant named Ashish Sarin. He had not been able to do well academically but I could see the passion in his eyes. He somehow reminded me of my younger self and we took him on board too.

Often, one has to set aside all written norms when it comes to building teams and go with their gut feeling.

My next priority was to find an expert in marketing (sales and leasing) as the team had zero experience in this crucial field. So we placed a small advertisement in the newspapers calling out for candidates. Amongst the many who applied was Pankaj Pal. He had a degree in architecture from the Indian Institute of Technology, Kharagpur.

At that time he was working with Eros, another builder. He was in the planning department and said that his job merely involved adding colour to sketches. He found this menial task very frustrating. However, he had had the chance to observe the marketing and sales department at close quarters and found its functions fascinating.

Conventional wisdom suggested we shouldn't hire him. Marketing is a specialized job and requires people who have been trained in the craft. Yet, there was something about Pal that made us hire him. In hindsight, it was one of the best choices I made.

In the years that followed, I saw this trend time and again. In fact, several forward-looking companies encourage such cross-function movements. It has some major benefits.

One, a person from a totally different stream brings a whole new perspective to the function. Teams that work in silos often fail to see their work from the others' point of view. Forming cross-functional teams is a good way to break this inertia. Two, it leads to innovative problem-solving. For the individual too, such cross-border functions can prove very helpful. There are times when he may feel pigeonholed in a role. The person stands to benefit in a totally new role as it throws up varied challenges, giving him a chance to reinvent himself. It also helps him broaden his horizons.

In Pal's case, he was an expert in architecture; this job allowed him to add marketing to his skill set. It raised his status in the market. This is why hiring Pal as our head of marketing made sense—both for the company as well as for him.

The timely completion of the Great Eastern Plaza and the deal with Ericsson gave our reputation a huge boost. People associated our company with clean, ethical practices and one that would stick to the deadlines promised.

We were a highly motivated team; we were extremely passionate about doing business in the real estate sector in a different way. The Great Eastern Shipping Company had given us a free hand and only asked us to think out of the box while working on our projects.

We had hired the best architects and contractors in our first project, we were personally involved in getting the titles from the Delhi Development Authority and we proved ourselves by delivering the Great Eastern Plaza within record time.

People had initially scoffed at us and had said we would have to pay bribes to get the approvals because that was how the sector worked. Being an ethical company, we never dealt with cash transactions—either with the government or with the buyers.

The Great Eastern Shipping Company was very charged with the success of the first project. It was not that big a project, but the directors of the company were upbeat and said we should work on more projects.

When we were working on the Bhikaji Cama Place project, a lot of information technology companies were coming into the country. The world had discovered the transformative capabilities of India's IT workforce. A large number of these companies needed office space.

Many of these overseas companies, unlike their Indian counterparts, were under strict watch for good corporate practices. They could not be seen providing a shabby work environment for their Indian employees.

It occurred to me that the work in such companies could get very monotonous, which would result in a high employee turnover. In such a scenario, companies need to spend a lot on training, which, in turn, would eat into their wafer-thin profit margins. One way out is to have a swanky office and the very best manpower practices, which would make employees think twice before jumping ship. This enhances engagement and creates some loyalty among employees.

Also, large corporations don't want to be perceived as bad employers in overseas markets. They try to maintain homogeneity in work cultures across continents.

Thus, the demand for good-quality real estate was on the rise. The problem was that there was no legitimate parcel of land in the capital that could match international standards. All the buildings in Connaught Place, the central business district of New Delhi at that time, had been sold to a large number of people. Anybody who had to hire a large space would have to negotiate with dozens, possibly hundreds, of owners. It was a marathon task for the real estate consultant to get the permission from all the owners to give office space to one person.

No state-of-the-art building with 100 per cent power back-up existed. During those days, it was normal to have power cuts for six to eight hours. People in offices had no option but to sweat it out in the summers.

The other reason that Delhi didn't have great commercial space was that the city was never the trade capital of the country. Though families like Shriram, Modi and Nanda had headquarters here, most of the big groups chose to operate out of Mumbai and Kolkata. Once the Naxal problem erupted in West Bengal, many of them relocated to Mumbai. Most business groups just maintained a liaison office in Delhi.

Nehru Place was set up in the 1980s in south Delhi to house offices as well as shops. While Connaught Place was the city's central business district, places like Nehru Place, Bhikaji Cama Place and Janakpuri were developed to meet the growing demand for commercial real estate.

However, these places had degenerated quickly to become urban slums. Several buildings in these areas posed huge security hazards in case there was a fire or some other calamity.

Though several companies like Ranbaxy, Apollo Tyres and Modi Rubber had their offices in Nehru Place, they soon became embarrassed to operate out of this area. Most of them had frequent visitors from overseas—bringing them here would create a bad impression. In contrast, we had created a building that was 100 per cent self-contained. Even if power and water supplies were disrupted, the building could run without a glitch round the clock because it boasted of its own power plant and water storage tanks. So, we thought we could help re-construct Nehru Place.

The demand was there—all you needed was the right piece of land. We could have acquired private land, but we found that in most cases the title deeds were not clear. We did not want to get involved in a property that was already under litigation. The problem we had encountered earlier resurfaced.

The only option left for us was to once again go for land auctioned by the Delhi Development Authority (DDA). There were a couple of vacant plots left in Nehru Place which were being used as garbage dumps.

DDA decided to auction these plots in 1996. When we went to see that property, we were in two minds because it was surrounded by a massive slum.

It was an opportunity but also a challenge. We were so charged up that we decided to bid for one of the plots, hoping the authorities would soon remove the slum cluster in front of the land.

However, we were not able to secure that particular parcel of land. Somebody had bid Rs. 28 crore and bagged the plot. But this person couldn't pay the money within the deadline. The Delhi Development Authority took the land back and decided to auction it once again, this time through a closed tender.

Sensing the general interest of builders, the DDA raised the reserve price to Rs. 30 crore. But we had done our homework this time. We quoted Rs. 35 crore and won the bid.

We started to plan another masterpiece. The Great Eastern Plaza at Bhikaji Cama Place was nearing completion and Ericsson was doing the interiors. We had a benchmark for quality. Having delivered a world-class project in record time, we couldn't let things slip in our second venture. Otherwise, we ran the risk of becoming a one-hit wonder. That would have eroded our credibility and dashed our hopes of becoming a noteworthy player in the premium segment of the market. Rivals too were watching us closely, some in anticipation that we would trip on the deadline this time. We decided to name this building the Great Eastern Centre and, once again, we hired the best architects and constructors to work for us. We removed 200 trucks of garbage after we took over the property from the DDA, and committed to deliver the project in eighteen months' time.

The Great Eastern Centre was a low-rise building. Once completed, it was quickly recognized as the best commercial building in the capital. It attracted clients like Microsoft, Cisco, Intel and Heinz Ketchup. All Fortune 500 companies that were coming into the country and wanted world-class office space sought us out.

Even other builders realized that we had brought about a shift in the way the market functioned.

This is when DLF Centre in Connaught Place, Berjaya House in New Friends Colony and Capital Court in Munirka came up. They learnt from our success that there was a market for top-end commercial space, provided all the laws and ethics were followed.

But the law of perfect competition was catching up with us and the market had turned soft. We wanted to lease out the Great Eastern Centre at $5 (Rs. 175 at the exchange rate prevailing at that time) a square foot.

Now, we knew that the market would not support such high rentals. We were also practical enough to realize that with the slum around the building, we would never be able to get premium rents (the slums were removed after the completion of the building). At the same time, we didn't want to keep the Great Eastern Centre waiting for too long because there was a high cost attached to it.

So we quickly lowered our expectations to a realistic level and leased out the building at $3 a square foot. By the end of day one, we were 100 per cent leased out—all 60,000 square feet. Capital Court and Berjaya House, which were still leasing out their property at $4–5 a square foot, had to sit idle for almost two years. Finally, they had to lease it out at rates not very different from ours.

The cost of constructing an A-class building in those days used to cost more or less Rs. 2,000 to Rs. 2,500 a square foot. Most builders at that time were doing commercial space at Rs. 800 to Rs. 1,000 a square foot. Our costs were higher because we provided central air conditioning and 100 per cent power backup.

We had completed the Great Eastern Plaza at Rs. 2,000 a square foot. The cost of the Nehru Place building was higher at almost Rs. 2,500 a square foot. There had been some inflation in the years in between. Also, this was open on all four sides, so the finishing area was a lot more.

The development cost came to Rs. 13–14 crore. Combined with the land cost of Rs. 35 crore, we had spent close to Rs 50 crore on the project. And we had leased it out at Rs. 125 per square foot per month. So we got Rs. 75 lakh as monthly rental—which meant an annual income of Rs. 9 crore. This was a tremendous return of 18 per cent.

The returns may have been handsome but it showed us that the market was really thin at that time: Just four or five constructions had brought rentals crashing by 40 per cent.

That's because there were very few multinational corporations in Delhi back then. While the demand was turning weak, land prices were sky-high owing to scarcity of supply. This meant that rents would also shoot up.

A lot of companies had started to look for commercial space in suburbs like Noida and Gurgaon in order to save money. Many organizations started maintaining only a small front-end office in Delhi and moved their back-end operations to these suburbs. In the years to come, these front-end offices would also vanish. Companies moved to the suburbs lock, stock and barrel.

We read the writing on the wall early. The opportunities in Delhi were few. The Berjaya Group of Malaysia, which operates across sectors like real estate, financial services and foods, had entered the market, and others were bound to follow, which had made bidding extremely competitive. The lease rentals were no longer in sync with the land prices. We too had bid for the Berjaya property but lost it.

The future clearly lay in the suburbs. We had acquired a property in Gurgaon earlier. It was one acre of land. The basic approvals were all there.

Like in Delhi, we wanted to do something extraordinary in Gurgaon. If this suburb was to become the future of Delhi, common sense dictated we announce our arrival with a bang. After all, in Nehru Place, we had made a world-class building on what was essentially a garbage dump. So we started making a commercial building which would have close to 1,00,000 square feet of space. It was significantly bigger than the other two projects we had completed earlier. We hired the architect group Rajendra Kumar & Associates for this property as well.

Soon, the building started to take shape. Because of its size, we decided to sell it in small portions. We did not want to lease it out because a large chunk of money would get blocked. We could not afford to do this since our budget was limited. It was very difficult to convince the market that we wanted to sell at a premium and all in white.

That, in fact, was the trend in 1996–1997—all-white deals simply didn't happen in real estate. The premium was essential because our construction cost was on the higher side: around Rs. 1,800 per square foot.

At that time, Motorola was looking to consolidate its offices in Delhi, just like Microsoft and Ericsson had done earlier. It had many offices all over the city; now, it wanted to bring all of them under one roof. Pankaj Pal and I went to talk to the local executives in Motorola.

They told us that the real estate aspect of the company was led by an American gentleman called Bob Tamborski. He was coming to India the next week to set up the company's Surya Sofitel office in south Delhi.

We went to meet him at the appointed time. Our sales pitch was fairly straightforward: we had Ericsson as a tenant and several top names from the world of business were moving into our second building in Nehru Place. We were fairly confident that these were good names to drop and would do the trick.

We were in for a shock. Tamborski was very no-nonsense and plainly said that we didn't have enough credentials and therefore, should not waste his precious time. Feeling snubbed, we decided to leave. But he got a call just then. We heard him say that he was staying at the Hyatt.

We sensed an opportunity here. I told him that he could see our showcase property, the Great Eastern Plaza, since it was a stone's throw from his hotel and then decide for himself. He relented and asked us to meet him at 8.00 a.m. the next morning.

In hindsight, it is clear to me that he didn't take us seriously because he had allotted us all of fifteen minutes to show him our property—it was impossible to walk down to our building, inspect it, and return to the hotel in that time. His brusque attitude could have made any other builder run away. Perhaps, he didn't expect us to take up the challenge.

For us, it was the opportunity of a lifetime. We reached the Hyatt at 7.45 a.m. Tamborski came down to the lobby at 8.00 a.m.

sharp. Without wasting any time on pleasantries, we started for the Great Eastern Plaza.

I started telling him about our building on the way, knowing very well that we only had limited time on our hands. I told him about the Italian marble flooring and the Belgian glass we had used, hoping to impress him with the expensive frills. The effect was just the opposite. Irritated, he said, 'This is your problem, you focus on unimportant things . . . We have not come all the way from the US to stand on Italian marble and to stare at Belgian glass.' He was almost screaming now. 'We want to do business. Where is the infrastructure? Everybody knows power cuts is a huge problem. What have you done to address it?'

As soon as we reached the building, we took him straight to the basement where our infrastructure plant was located. This changed everything. Tamborski started talking excitedly and questioned us relentlessly for the next forty-five minutes.

It was clear that he had forgotten about his next meeting. He was as chirpy as a child and said this was exactly what he had been looking for all these days. He called Amit Sharma, the then country head of Motorola, and told him that after wasting two years, he had finally found what he had in mind.

We fixed the next meeting at The Oberoi. Col. Sodhi and Pal were there with me. We quickly made our presentation. Seven different business groups of Motorola were present there. Things were going fine and everybody was enthusiastic—till we showed them the location of the building on the map.

Instantly, almost all of the local staff was up in arms. The land was at Sukhrali village on the road to old Gurgaon. There were crater-like potholes on the road, some up to two feet deep. Not one of the Motorola executives wanted to travel on that road. They all knew its pitiable condition. They told Tamborski that this location wouldn't work.

I suspect many of them lived in south Delhi and were reluctant to commute daily to Gurgaon—that too, to a distant part of it.

After fifteen minutes of chaos, Tamborski got up and said this was going to be his last visit to India. 'In the last two years, I have seen each and every developer, and each and every site in India, but I have failed to find office space for you. This location is secondary and the road is bad, which might make your daily commute longer by ten minutes, but you people say that you work for sixteen hours in a day. According to me, these are the people who can give you the right environment for those sixteen hours. So if this is not good enough for you, goodbye,' he said.

Everybody sat down. The loud protests had subsided.

The next day, they all fell in line. Tamborski was not oblivious to their anxiety and told us to keep trying to get the local authorities to improve the road.

He specified the infrastructure that was required for employees to work for long hours. We sold the building to Motorola for Rs. 40 crore. It was the biggest commercial real estate deal in Gurgaon at that time.

Tamborski was a hard taskmaster. He had laid down tough ground rules for us. If we did not complete the building in the time frame specified by him, he would levy a penalty of Rs. 1 lakh per day on us. He also said payments would be tied to the milestones of the project: only after we achieved the target, would the promised money be paid to us.

I told him that without some money upfront it would be difficult for us to construct the office. So he said he would give us a letter of credit from ANZ Grindlays Bank. Soon, we got Rs. 7 crore from the bank.

I found the project exciting and my confidence was soaring. Before we signed on the dotted line, I extracted a promise from Tamborski: if we completed the project before time, he would give us a bonus equivalent to the penalty of Rs. 1 lakh per day he had specified. He agreed sportingly. The deadline for completing the project was sixteen months; we delivered it with almost a month to go and collected our bonus.

The Motorola Asia chief came in and said that was the best Motorola building in the entire continent. His words were a huge boost to our confidence.

The total cost of construction was around Rs. 20 crore, and the land would have cost close to Rs. 5 crore. We had sold it to Motorola for Rs. 40 core. That was a neat profit of 60 per cent.

Working with Tamborski was a great learning experience for us. It was tough because he was involved in almost all aspects of the construction—from safety, quality to labour facilities. He was an excellent, very intelligent technocrat from whom we learnt quite a lot. We have hardly met after that, but the impact he left on me was indelible.

After we had completed the Great Eastern Plaza and Great Eastern Centre, we realized that there was no proper company in the country that dealt with facility management. Constructing buildings was fine, but they needed to be maintained and run properly. This required special skills.

It began to dawn on us that there were a number of modern buildings around—and more were coming up—which threw up great business opportunities for facility management. But we did not have the required skills. It was decided that we should enter the business with a foreign partner.

After looking at various options, we decided to engage with Knight Frank of London. One of the biggest names in the business, it was founded in 1896. Currently, it has over 335 offices in fifty-two countries, employing more than 12,000 professionals.

Sometime in 1995–96, Sheth, Col. Sodhi and I went to London to initiate talks with the company. Its office was located on the busy Baker Street, famous for being home to Sherlock Holmes. We met their senior staff. After our visit, some of its top executives came to India. They were quite impressed with our development plans, though there was one crucial difference: while in London, a great deal of the infrastructure was provided by the city, here it was made available by the builder.

The talks proved to be successful. And that's how Knight Frank India was born, a company owned equally by Knight Frank and the Great Eastern Shipping Company.

Around this time, the great dotcom boom was in its nascent stages. The internet, it was felt, would change the way we live. Indians, given their aptitude for software, took to the internet like fish to water. Silicon Valley, the biggest home to start-ups in the world, was dominated by what came to be called the Indian Internet Mafia—such was their control of the industry.

The possibilities the internet presented were indeed huge. At the click of a button, all sorts of information was available to people. Entrepreneurs, young and old, rushed headlong into it. The financiers of the world were fascinated by it. Venture capitalists and other private equity funds came to India by the dozen. Money was there for the asking, and due diligence norms were conveniently forgotten in the euphoria. Some deals were concluded in less than an hour's time.

Many did not have a credible business plan. But that didn't seem to matter—the name of the game was valuation. Start-ups found it incredibly easy to raise money from the stock market; many funds, while the going was good, made a neat pile of money.

A byproduct of this boom was that it launched an entrepreneurial wave in India. Before this, it was unimaginable to enter business with just intellectual capital. Up until then, there were only brick and mortar businesses, and they required money. In the internet age, the entry barriers came crashing down.

In a sense, it led to the democratization of business. No longer did one need to be born into a rich family to get into business. A small amount of money was enough to get you started in life. Indeed, some of the internet giants of today were incubated in garages and hostel rooms. If you had a good idea, there were enough people out there who were willing to invest in it.

In fact, such was the euphoria that even ideas that were only partially ready got easy money in those days.

When the dotcom boom was at its peak in 1999, Pal and I used to discuss often about how the internet could be used in the real estate sector. We were both working for the Great Eastern Shipping Company at that time, but that didn't stop us from talking about our entrepreneurial dreams.

We saw an inspiration when the Times Group invested in Magic Bricks, a property portal. That got us thinking: we needed a solid business proposition, with the internet as the enabler. We knew one thing then—people weren't ready to buy property online at that time.

Most Indians buy a house once or twice in their lifetimes. It is a momentous decision taken after a great deal of physical verification. But the internet offered the opportunity to process this information in a more effective way. We used this as the core idea around which we built our business plans.

Though we were extremely enthusiastic about our venture, we knew that it was safe to only work on it after office hours. Somehow, the idea of giving up our jobs to pursue this dream full-time did not appeal to us. We told ourselves that if it took off then we would quit the company. We were taking a calculated risk.

We designed it as a brick and mortar business, not as a pure internet-based company. While everyone around us was very taken in by internet, we knew it wasn't an end in itself but rather a tool that made doing business (through quick access to information) easier.

After much deliberation, we registered a domain name called Property Exchange to give shape to our entrepreneurial dreams. For shares and securities, there was the stock exchange. For commodities, there was the commodity exchange. Could there be a similar internet-based business model in real estate?

We knew that real estate would never be transacted the way shares are traded on the stock exchange—it requires very careful investing. But there is one similarity: underlying all trades on the stock exchange is a security paper, just like there is a title deed for every property which is bought and sold. And just like a security is a certified document, shouldn't every property that comes up for (offline) trade carry a similar certificate?

This, we felt, would increase the confidence of buyers and would give more depth to the real estate market. The other similarity is that brokers are important for the share market as well as the real estate market—an inescapable part of the food chain.

We decided to get on board a legal expert who would do the due diligence on the properties. Our website, would have properties listed on it. The moment a buyer clicked on a property, a communication would go out to the designated broker in the area directly who would carry out a physical inspection. Another communication would go to the legal expert who would give you a title certificate on that property saying this property was fit and there were no hurdles.

We thought this would bridge the huge trust deficit in the market. We began to imagine of a time when no property in the country was bought or sold unless it was certified by Property Exchange.

The concept was very good. But to get started, we needed money. So we made a business plan. We spoke to a number of prospective investors. Citibank was keen to invest. We even had a meeting with its representatives.

But then, without any of us anticipating it, the dotcom bubble burst. Investors developed cold feet almost overnight. Nobody wanted to touch new economy stocks in the market. In no time, internet entrepreneurs had turned from celebrities to outcasts.

Unfortunately, all the people we had spoken to thought that Property Exchange was just another dotcom company and were, therefore, reluctant to open their purse strings for us. It was difficult for us to make them see reason.

Most of the evaluators were not from the real estate sector and hence, did not understand what we had in mind. In our model, we were out to address a basic problem in the market and the internet was just a tool. It was not about online transactions. That was never on our mind.

However hard we tried to defend our product, it fell on deaf ears. That was the end of it.

But it was heartening for us to see traces of our business plans in some of the new websites that came up in later years. We had circulated our presentation very extensively—to almost twenty investment bankers. It had perhaps found its way to others.

With investment worth Rs. 20 crore, we had set out to do business worth a billion dollars through Property Exchange. Just like the membership of the Bombay Stock Exchange was being sold at that time for Rs. 1 crore, we had decided to charge each property broker Rs. 10 lakh to register on our website.

There were several queries. We told brokers that they could recover the money from sub-brokers—by making them a part of the network. We thought of designing signboards outside the offices of brokers—that they were members of Property Exchange.

We just had the business plan. We never implemented it.

Meanwhile, at the Great Eastern Shipping Company, life was about to take an unexpected turn. And the man who was all set to turn our world upside down came from an old business family in Delhi.

Ramkrishna Dalmia (1893–1978) had a chequered life. At one time, he was India's third-richest industrialist after J.R.D. Tata and Ghanshyam Das Birla. He was also a media mogul, self-proclaimed expert on international affairs, protector of the holy cow and husband to no less than six wives.

The man had his admirers—and his detractors.

'He is an ugly man with an ugly face and an ugly mind and an ugly heart,' Jawaharlal Nehru once said of him. The two had never seen eye to eye. In 1931, when Motilal Nehru died, Dalmia sent Nehru Rs. 5,000 to tide over the crisis. Nehru, who had become an avowed socialist by then, refused the help but offered to distribute the money amongst the poor.

Dalmia, according to one account, later invested Rs. 10,000 for a 30 per cent stake in Nehru's newspaper, *National Herald*—which finds itself at the centre of a major political controversy now. Both of them put their sons-in-law, Sahu Shanti Prasad Jain and Feroze Gandhi, respectively, on the newspaper's board of directors. The venture required more and more money. Nehru and Dalmia began to bicker. Ultimately, Dalmia left in a huff.

Subsequently, Dalmia blamed Nehru for the plight of Hindus during Partition. This piqued Nehru, independent India's first prime minister.

More was to come. Dalmia's astrologer had told him that he would become the finance minister of the country; emboldened, he stepped up his attack against Nehru. He even used the newspaper he had bought, the *Times of India*, to settle scores with the prime minister. The rift between the two men widened.

The same astrologer had said that the Soviet Union would dump currency into India and plunge the country into an economic crisis. Dalmia began to sell his stock, often at a pittance. Around this time, it also came to light that he had taken out public money from his insurance company for speculation. He had spent two years in jail for this misdemeanour.

In sharp contrast, his younger brother, Jaidayal Dalmia (1904–1993), was a saintly person. He set up many charitable trusts that ran hospitals, schools, dharamshalas and so on. He was a vocal social reformer and a lifelong supporter of the movement to ban cow slaughter.

One of his sons, Ajay Hari Dalmia, worked with the family-controlled Orissa Cements till he decided to branch out on his own in 1999. He had two sons, Abhishek and Chaitanya. It was Abhishek Dalmia who shook up things at the Great Eastern Shipping Company.

It so happened that the real estate business had to be separated from the Great Eastern Shipping Company. That's because the International Finance Corporation, the private sector lending arm of the World Bank, had bought a stake in the company and the rules did not allow foreign investment in real estate. As a result, the real estate division was branded to become a separate company called Gesco Corporation.

Its shareholding mirrored that of the Great Eastern Shipping Company. Ghanshyam Sheth was its managing director and Sudhir Mulji was its chairman.

Meanwhile, Abhishek Dalmia, a chartered accountant by training, had set up Renaissance, a firm loosely modelled on Warren Buffet's Berkshire Hathaway.

In fact, he was a fan of the legendary investor and a shareholder in his company. He once even travelled thirty hours to Omaha in the United States to attend the annual general meeting of the shareholders of Berkshire Hathaway. 'To my mind, Buffet is living proof that good guys do not always finish last. His ethical standards are legendary. He has no ego at all (despite his achievements) and has consciously cultivated a low profile. If you hop into a cab in Omaha and ask to be driven to Buffet's house, chances are that you will be asked to provide the address,' he wrote in *Business Today* in 2004.

Like Buffet, Abhishek Dalmia started to watch out for undervalued stocks and companies where promoters had a low stake and were, hence, susceptible to a takeover.

Gesco Corporation was a sitting duck. The Sheth family's stake was probably in the low double digits and the share price too was low—it had hovered between Rs. 10 and Rs. 15 for a long time in spite of the projects we had executed.

But there was a reason behind these low prices. Till the mid-1980s, Indian businessmen were happy to run their businesses with a very small stake. There was punitive taxation and businessmen routinely sold shares to meet their tax liabilities. Hostile takeovers were unheard of. And businessmen knew that state-owned financial institutions and banks, which had come to acquire stakes in a large number of companies by converting their loans into equity, could be relied upon for support in case of such hostility.

Thus, the Birla family owned more of Tata Steel than Tata Sons at one time.

But businessmen were shaken out of their comfort zone in the mid-1980s when Swraj Paul, a non-resident Indian, attempted to take over Escorts from Har Prasad Nanda and Delhi Cloth Mills (it was subsequently renamed DCM) from two brothers—Bharat Ram and Charat Ram.

The Indian promoters, much to their chagrin, found the banks and financial institutions had actually begun to lean on

Paul. Finally, Paul had to give up the bid after Rajiv Gandhi intervened on behalf of the two Indian business houses.

The episode did serve to expose the danger businessmen faced and the urgent need to shore up their stakes. Most businessmen started to do that right away. However, the Sheth family had not protected Gesco Corporation properly.

Abhishek Dalmia quietly bought a 10.5 per cent stake in the company.

Under the rules laid down by the Securities and Exchange Board of India, the stock market regulator, he was required to make an open offer the moment his stake hit 15 per cent. He didn't wait for that and immediately announced that he was ready to buy another 45 per cent stake in Gesco Corporation at Rs. 23 a share—he subsequently raised his bid to Rs. 27 a share.

The Sheths finally began to pull their act together. Family friend Deepak Parekh, the chairman of Housing Development Finance Corporation and easily the country's best-known corporate troubleshooter, brought in Anand Mahindra, the chairman of Mahindra & Mahindra. The real estate arm Mahindra Realty & Infrastructure was going to be the white knight.

Together, they made a counter offer for 33.5 per cent of Gesco Corporation at Rs. 44 a share. Finally, in a deal brokered by S. Gurumurthy (the famous Chennai-based chartered accountant), Abhishek Dalmia sold his stake to the Sheth–Mahindra combine.

I never met Abhishek Dalmia. But my friends who knew him well always held his business instincts in the highest regard. Dalmia, who used to sport a *choti*, the way pious Hindus do, and was known to be religious, used to work out of his office in Connaught Place. Some found him ruthlessly ambitious, while others claimed that he was just a publicity hound.

The war, though it was short-lived, was over. Abhishek Dalmia had made a handsome profit. And the control of Gesco

Corporation moved from the Sheths to Mahindra. He merged his realty division with it and the company became Mahindra Gesco.

The understanding was that Mahindra Gesco would be run by Sheth as the managing director. Anand Mahindra may become the chairman, and Mulji may remain as the vice-chairman. But the cultures of the two groups were very different. At that time, the practice in the Mahindra companies was to set up committees. In the Great Eastern Shipping Company, there was 100 per cent delegation of power and very little bureaucracy. We used to discuss the projects with Sheth directly and then go ahead with the work.

In the Mahindra group, there were several layers of bureaucracy that each proposal had to pass through; this took a lot of time and a whole lot of proposals died along the way.

Cultural mismatch is often the biggest problem with mergers and acquisitions. Aided by smart investment bankers and lawyers, businessmen often wrap up deals quickly but forget to address a prominent soft issue—cultural integration. Research shows that almost 80 per cent of the mergers fail in this aspect. As a result, synergy seldom results from such mergers.

It is now recommended that only those companies with cultural similarities should merge. The employees of the acquired company often worry about the merger and the resultant practices. These concerns need to be addressed to the acquirer. In case the cultures of the merging entities are completely different, it makes sense for the acquirer not to interfere too much in the affairs of the acquired company.

Still, we went about with business as usual. Then, one day, a proposal came from the Bakshi family. They are an old family with substantial interests in real estate. They owned companies like Oriental Infrastructure and Continental Engines.

One of their directors, Kanwal Jeet Singh Bakshi, nicknamed Kummy, called to say the family wanted to enter a joint venture with us. 'I have been able to consolidate fourteen acres of land in Gurgaon. I have the licence to develop it into a gated community. You have a good reputation in the market, let us enter a joint venture,' he said.

The land was right next to the DLF Golf Course—a prime piece of real estate, by any standard.

All I could say was that I had to first forward the proposal to the Mahindra headquarters in Mumbai, though I suspected that the group would not be interested in a joint venture. But Bakshi was very keen and wanted to work with us.

I told him off the cuff that we could execute the project by lending our expertise to it and help create brand equity by stepping into the owner's shoes, provided they were willing to make the investment. We would manage the project right from its conceptualization, to building it, selling it and ensure it is handed over to the consumers—all for a 'success fee' of 10 per cent of the top line. I told him it was nothing. 'We have studied your project in the market. You got the licence six months ago; then you tried to launch it in the market, but you have not been able to sell even six apartments. You are selling it at Rs. 1,600 a square foot; we shall sell it at Rs. 1,800 a square foot,' I said, brimming with confidence. 'Even if you pay us 10 per cent, which is Rs. 180 per square foot, you will still get better money and faster sales.'

He started laughing. The next day, Bakshi called me at 7.30 a.m. and asked me to meet him for breakfast at the Hyatt. He said: 'Your idea of managing the project has appealed to me. Let's work on this. You charge 8 per cent since all the approvals are in place and the project is ready to take off.'

We decided to make a proposal and send it to our head office in Mumbai.

As I thought about it, the possibilities this project presented began to excite me. I told Pal, my sounding board for all new business plans, that we should develop it into a proper business model. We would draw the concept, do the construction, and take care of marketing, accounting and documentation for a fee. Except buying the land and providing the money, we would do everything that is done in the real estate sector.

The idea appealed to him. We started putting a model together. We called it REAM: Real Estate Asset Management. We drafted everything—the management review committee, job responsibilities et cetera. Finally, after much brainstorming, we were able to put together a business model that allowed us execute the project without any significant investment on our part.

We went to meet Arun Nanda, who was in charge of the Mahindra realty business, with the proposal. He saw merit in our argument: no investment was needed and the team was already in place. So he asked us to go ahead.

We signed an agreement with the Bakshi family and got to work on the Central Park project. All work was done by us. In fact, I even designed the Central Park logo. Once again, we hired Rajendra Kumar & Associates as the architects of the project.

I convinced Rajendra Kumar that we should also have an international architect as a partner in the venture. This was an upscale residential project. We were well-established in the commercial real estate; now, if we wanted to earn a name for ourselves in residential real estate as well, we would have to create something that was way ahead of our rivals.

Rahul, Kumar's son, agreed and we travelled to Singapore and shortlisted some architects. Finally, SAA Partners was selected.

In Singapore, instead of a mock-up flat, they set up mock-up pavilions—a complete lobby-to-tower experience, along with the fully furnished flats.

Central Park became the biggest real estate success in Gurgaon at that time. All the big developers came to see it, including the Chandras of Unitech and the Singhs of DLF with their teams. I overheard some women saying they were ready to sell their jewellery to buy an apartment here.

The average price of an apartment was close to Rs. 2,000 a square foot—a record at that time. There were 413 flats in Central Park, and all of them got sold out.

The total built-up area of Central Park was 1.2 million square feet. We made Rs. 20 crore on that project. Our investment was only our manpower.

In spite of this success, I realized that not much was moving at Mahindra. It was time for me to part ways with the company.

The word got around and a lot of people approached the senior team at the company. Mohit Gujral, the famous architect, took Col. Sodhi and me to meet Rajiv Singh of DLF. He asked us to join him, not in DLF but in a boutique company, with great salaries.

We agreed but told him that if we started an independent venture, we would require equity in it. Singh said he had never given the equity option to anyone but could consider profit-sharing. We almost agreed. Gujral was also to be a part of that setup. We withdrew at the last stage because of our parallel discussions with the Bakshis.

In fact, the Bakshis were very keen to work with us. They had enough land bank—four million square feet on Sohna Road alone. Kummy Bakshi offered to make me the managing director and also threw in equity in the deal.

Meanwhile, Sudhir Mulji too had liked our REAM model. It meant going asset-light, which meant it was not capital-intensive. The risk was low. He must have spoken of it to others.

One day, Sheth came to Delhi and asked to meet us over lunch at the Radisson, Delhi. He told us that we had done good work in residential as well as commercial real estate and had hit upon a good business model. He exhorted us to set up our own business using the REAM model.

But we had no money, we told him. How would we pay salaries? Who would pay the rent for our offices?

He spoke to Sudhir Mulji who said: 'We will pay the money for salaries, just start it.' Sheth spoke to the Choudhries, a well-established business family with interests in hospitality and healthcare in India and abroad, who had land bank and had shown interest in doing business together. So the money was contributed by Sudhir Mulji, Ghanshyam Sheth and the Choudhries.

At this time, Arun Nanda at Mahindra, a veteran of over twenty-five years in the group, had come to know that I was preparing to leave. He thought that the reason for my exit was the fact that Col. Sodhi was my superior—which was certainly not the case. I had always treated him as my mentor. Nanda invited me over to Mumbai quite a few times and said that Col. Sodhi would retire soon and I could take his place. He even offered to make me the CEO of Mahindra World City in Chennai and raise my salary significantly.

But I had made up my mind. I had a good relationship with Sheth and Mulji, not to mention Col. Sodhi. A known person is always better than an unknown one.

The Choudhrie family too was not unknown to us. We had recommended a few contractors to them when they were setting up Ananda in the Himalayas, a spa resort above Rishikesh. Singapore Technologies had been our associate at the Great Eastern Shipping Company.

On our recommendation, Singapore Technologies and a local contractor took up the construction. However, the two ran into some problems. The Choudhries said that since we had referred the contractors, we should become the arbitrator. That contractor, R.K. Arora, would eventually become a top developer and his company, Supertech, would put up ambitious projects in Delhi's suburbs (in his heyday, he had even thought of starting an airline!).

So I decided to go with Sheth and Mulji's suggestion. Our decision annoyed Bakshi as well as Rajiv Singh, and I think Arun Nanda also, at least to an extent. But one has to make such choices in life. It is difficult to keep everybody happy.

The investors agreed to give us—Col. Sodhi, myself and three other colleagues—20 per cent equity, and Rs. 15 crore as seed capital. Sheth and Mulji owned 20 per cent of the equity capital each, while the Choudhries too took 20 per cent each.

The equity capital was meant to pay our salaries for a couple of years, by which time the business should be able to sustain itself.

Our mandate was to look for projects according to the Central Park model: REAM.

We all left Mahindra Gesco and registered as Alpha G Corp. The Choudhries had a business called Alpha in the UK. They liked to use Alpha in all their ventures. Sheth, after separating from Mahindra, had set up G Corp which was active in the west and the south. Hence, we settled on the name Alpha G Corp.

We rented our first office space—5, Aradhana Enclave, a residential double-storey bungalow in south Delhi.

5

Venture Shastra

The money that the shareholders had given us was like seed capital—it wasn't enough for us to have launched ourselves in the market with a bang. There was no way we could have bought land and started a grand project with such little money. Conventionally, real estate has always been a highly capital-intensive sector. Some builders get over this problem by joining hands with brokers, but we were very clear that we didn't want to go down this road.

We were also very charged up. We had big dreams and we were determined to transform them into reality. This was our chance to prove that our earlier successes were not just flukes.

As it is, our business model, Real Estate Asset Management, did not require a great deal of capital. We were convinced that the market was ready to accept our idea.

The fact that our capital was rather modest reflected in our choice of office. After looking at various options, we settled for 5, Aradhana Enclave because at Rs. 1,50,000 per month, it was the cheapest office space we could afford. From this flat in south Delhi, the journey of Alpha G Corp began.

We didn't have to look too far for our first project. The Choudhries, the largest shareholders in the company, owned close to ten acres of land in Sector 22 along the old Gurgaon highway. Much before the swanky highway connecting Delhi and Jaipur was built, this was the road people took to travel past Gurgaon.

But it happened to fall on what was considered the wrong side of the highway. While all the residential development was taking place on the other side, this land parcel was surrounded by industrial units, including the first factory of Maruti Suzuki—the country's largest car maker.

The Choudhries were finalizing a deal with Tata Housing. The idea was to construct houses for the low- and middle-income category of people. The location of the land was such that nobody could even dream of constructing an upscale residential project there. Arcorp, a Canadian firm of architects, had finished the initial design of the project.

We sensed that this was the opportunity we were looking for. We told the Choudhries that we would like to work on this project, and the commercial terms were of no consideration for us: whatever Tata Housing had offered, we were prepared to match it.

Everybody cautioned us saying that we were venturing into unfamiliar territory. While we had only worked on upscale projects so far, this was way down the value chain. The apartments, we were told, would have to be small—anywhere between 700 square feet and 1200 square feet—and would have to be priced competitively because the project fell bang in the middle of Udyog Vihar, the industrial township of Gurgaon.

There was a substantial degree of truth in what the naysayers were telling us. The infrastructure was poor, to say the least. As heavy trucks plied on the roads non-stop, they were in a major state of disrepair. The kind of buyers we had dealt with so far would think twice before driving down to even visit this site. So the opportunity to leverage our existing clientele to sell this project was almost zero. These were formidable obstacles, yet we felt that we would be able to overcome them and come out successful.

Looking back, I can say that it was a bold gamble on our part: an upscale gated community in an industrial area. Naturally, our pitch puzzled everybody. Some called us insane. Maybe we were being foolhardy, but at times such contrarian thinking helps.

This reminds me of the story of C.P. Krishnan Nair (1922–2014), fondly called Capt. Nair, the founder of Leela Hotels. He went against conventional wisdom more than once and always came out as a winner. When everybody was building hotels in south Mumbai, he opted for a site close to the airport. He was told that the hotel would never make profits, but the critics had to eat their words when it became a resounding success. People found it very convenient to stay in a hotel close to the airport.

When everybody was rushing to build in north Goa, he chose a location in south Goa to construct a hotel. His pitch was that the hotel was located far from the maddening crowds of north Goa and people loved it! And in Bangalore, he went for premium tariff. The naysayers said nobody would be willing to pay so much, but Bangalore soon emerged as India's answer to the Silicon Valley, attracting high-profile visitors from across the world. The demand for premium rooms shot through the roof and Capt. Nair's hunch was proved as right once again.

Capt. Nair had a great appetite for risk, plus an innate sense of what would work and what wouldn't. His biggest gamble, perhaps, was The Leela Chanakyapuri, which he built in the heart of Delhi at a cost of over Rs. 1500 crore. It was easily the most expensive hotel ever built in the country. Subsequently, the debt he had taken for the hotel began to hurt, and he had to look at ways to reduce it, which involved selling some properties. But what can be said without hesitation is that luck truly favours those who dare to take risks.

The Choudhries were our shareholders alright, but to expect them to hand over the project to us on a silver platter was unreasonable on our part. They were, at the end of the day, hardnosed businessmen. The only way we could get them to even consider our offer was to ensure our terms were better than what Tata Housing had provided.

When we were shown the term sheet they were signing with Tata Housing, we offered to work for a smaller cut.

In hindsight, it was the perfect entry strategy. Every business should always factor in the long-term benefits of their actions: do you want profits in the short-term or do you want to build your brand equity first and then leverage it for long-term profits?

We could have pestered the Choudhries to give us this project at the same terms as what Tata Housing had offered them, but this would have affected our long-term relationship with them. Moreover, the market would have taken a negative view of us— that we had pulled strings to bag the project and did not get it on merit. This would have affected our reputation in a major way. One often has to take such calls in business. In our case, it turned out to be the right decision.

The Choudhries agreed to our terms and conditions. In return, we asked that we be given a free hand to change the project plan. They readily consented to our demand.

One thing was clear to us right from the beginning: we were not going to build a low- or mid-income housing project here. It would have to be an upscale construction.

We had made a few mistakes when we had worked on Central Park, most notable of which was the size of the apartments. In those days, people who moved to Gurgaon from Delhi did so in the hope of moving to a more spacious house, especially bigger bedrooms. At Central Park, the bedrooms were smaller. They also had a common washroom, which was rather inconvenient for the residents. So, we decided that the houses in our new project would at least be of 2,400 square feet.

Another concern at Central Park was the cramped service areas: kitchen balcony, service balcony et cetera. In any modern household, there are a lot of appliances which the builder must account for and create adequate space. This was a factor we had overlooked at Central Park, but we were determined not to make the same mistake in the future.

We now had to sell our plan to the Choudhries. They saw merit in our argument and agreed to our suggestions. We decided to build 240 apartments on the ten acres of land. We named the project Gurgaon One. The name was meant to convey two things: one, it was in the heart of Gurgaon; and two, it was on top of the pecking order. We knew location was not on our side, so the name had to be chosen carefully.

Once our new plan was ready, I invited brokers over to get their feedback. In the market around Delhi, brokers are unavoidable accomplices in marketing any project. They have their own network of investors, who make their demands to the builders via the brokers. In a sense, they are the market makers for any project.

About thirty of them came to my office for the presentation. I apprised them of the plan. They heard me out patiently, but showed no sign of enthusiasm. 'Mr Sayal,' one of them said bluntly, 'You have tasted a great deal of success so far, but this plan sounds really far-fetched.'

I realized that the main problem most of them had was with the location of the project in Udyog Vihar.

Undeterred by their frank criticism, I said we hoped to create a unique project. One major positive factor, I told them, was that the project was next to an out-of-use ammunition dump, located over thousands of acres. Since no construction could ever take place there, the residents would have an unrestricted view of the greenery.

Even within the plot of Gurgaon One, there were a number of old trees we didn't want to cut. There was one banyan tree at a rather odd location. We uprooted it and successfully planted it nearby. I narrated this story to the brokers, but they refused to be moved.

Nevertheless, I invited them to visit the site for a guided tour that coming Saturday.

On that day, we erected a *shamiana* at the site and made arrangements for snacks and lunch. Our architects and consultants were all present, ready to answer any query the brokers might have. We had invited thirty-five brokers in all for the tour. Finally, only five or six of them trudged in. It was a poor show by any standard.

For a moment, I was assailed by grave self-doubt: were we on the right track, or had we bitten off more than we could chew? Over the next couple of hours, the architects and consultants walked these few brokers through the plan and designs. Whatever questions they had were all answered satisfactorily.

As the session progressed, I could sense the brokers' mood changing. They were very sceptical when they came in, but now their confidence in the project began to show. By the end of the tour, I knew we had managed to convince them.

As many as twenty-two apartments—almost 10 per cent of the total stock—were booked right then and there, even before all the revised approvals could be collected. Apart from the brokers, some of the architects and consultants also signed up for the apartments. Such was the enthusiasm!

The brokers who had turned up for the event managed to sell the entire project over the next two or three months. Those who had chosen to stay away later called me to express regret—they said they had made a huge mistake.

We had promised to complete the project in four years. We could have delivered earlier, but since most buyers had gone for a construction-linked payment plan, it would have an unnecessary financial stretch for them. We were able to hand over the apartments to the buyers well within the deadline.

In a market where delays were the norm, and not just an exception, we delivered Gurgaon One before time. One way we were able to do this was that we made sure that the money coming from the buyer would go straight into a specific retention and trust account, and the money required for the construction would get transferred into a separate expense account, which we would control.

We had insisted on this even when we had worked on Central Park. Since we had a bumper sale there and money was needed only in phases, we had a neat surplus in our kitty. Kummy Bakshi, the promoter of Central Park, told us he was paying 16 per cent interest to the banks in loans for other projects and he would be happy to pay us the same interest if we gave him Rs. 25 crore. We refused. 'This isn't your money,' we told him. 'It belongs to the buyers and we can't give it to you.'

It is a well-known fact that promoters often dip into their own companies' pockets for cash. This move exposes the company to a grave risk. It is the job of the custodian to see that money earmarked for a specific purpose, is spent only on that purpose and on nothing else. It may create some temporary bitterness, but it sends out a clear signal to the promoters and also the creditors. This financial discipline alone ensured that, like Central Park, we were able to complete Gurgaon One well within time.

Once again, we engaged top-notch people for Gurgaon One. Ahluwalia Constructions did all the civil work, while we retained Arcop as the architect. The firm had worked on several prestigious residential projects in Gurgaon, like ITC's Laburnum and Garden Estate.

There was close to a million square feet of development in Gurgaon One. The cost of building it was around Rs. 100 crore, and we made nearly Rs. 10 crore on the project. It met all our running expenses: thirty people, thirty computers, office space et cetera.

The Choudhries made good returns on their land. Since there was about a million square feet of construction, the average selling price was Rs. 2,100 per square foot. After accounting for the cost of land (around Rs. 20 crore), the cost of construction and our commission, they still made a neat profit.

We had proved the efficacy of our business model. Our ability to deliver projects on time was well established now. We now started to look for more projects to work on.

The successful execution of Gurgaon One had raised our profile in the market. The Choudhrie family began to view us with a great deal of respect. We had helped them monetize an asset quite well, and I was sure they were ready to give us more projects. In the market, word began to spread fast that we were reliable people who could get the job done properly and well within time.

The second opportunity came knocking on our doors soon enough. Rita Choudhrie, the wife of the late Rajiv Choudhrie (her daughter was married to Kamal Nath's son, Bakul Nath), owned a commercial building along Golf Course Road in Gurgaon. Unlike Gurgaon One, this was on the right side of the suburban city. There were glitzy offices and swanky flats all around. She asked us if we could help her refurbish the building and lease it out.

We asked her if we could take a look at the site first. When we got there, we were in for a rude shock. There was nothing more than a shell—it had a distinctively spooky feeling of a ghost town. It would take a lot of effort on our part to refurbish the building, but the location was absolutely terrific.

We began wondering why the building was not getting leased out. We approached the brokers, only to be told that they weren't prepared to touch it. They were somehow under the impression that the landlady wasn't really interested in leasing out the property. 'When we approach her with an offer to pay a rent of Rs. 28 (per square foot per month), she asks for Rs. 31. And when we go with an offer of Rs. 31, she demands Rs. 34,' one exasperated broker told me.

We decided to take up the challenge. Our first task was to complete the building. The shell looked very forbidding. There were at least a thousand bats living in the lift shafts. And when it rained, there was as much water inside the shell as there was outside. The building was as good as junk, we told Choudhrie without mincing words.

We asked her for six months to refurbish the building. After studying the market, we told her that it would be possible to rent out the space at Rs. 30 per square foot per month. If the offer was less than that, we said we would seek her permission; otherwise, we would need full power to lease out the space.

She agreed to our proposal. I guess she knew that she had nothing to lose here.

We were able to complete the civil work within six months. The bats had been driven away and the leakages had been fixed. We decided to call the project Golf View Corporate Tower because it overlooked the DLF Golf Course (in subsequent years, DLF built several tall buildings between Golf View Corporate Tower and the golf course. Now, only a slender view of the driveway can be seen, that too from my office on the sixth floor).

Once the refurbishment was complete, buyers started trickling in. Among the first tenants was an information technology company from the United States. It was all set to kick off its Indian operations and had agreed to take 15,000 square feet of space in Golf View Corporate Tower, spread over two floors.

We set a date for the promoter of the company, a non-resident Indian, to come in and sign the contract. On that date, we waited eagerly for him, but he showed no sign of arriving. Then, we saw two cars driving up to the gate. We could see the promoter in one car; he was sitting next to a man dressed in long robes. They were followed by another car. However, instead of turning into the driveway, the two cars stopped and then sped away from the gate. They never came inside.

We found this very strange and wondered what had gone wrong. In a little while, the gentleman called to say that he had been accompanied by his spiritual guru, who had rejected the building outright. Somehow, the guru had felt that there was an air of negativity about the project. Its edges were sharply cut and the façade was made of black granite, which had unnerved the holy man.

There was nothing we could do to salvage the deal. The guru, it was clear, had a very strong hold over his disciple. The agreement was called off.

We were very disappointed. Some began to wonder if the project was jinxed. A few suggested we get a *vastu shastra* expert to look at the building and suggest suitable changes.

Vastu shastra is the ancient Indian treatise on architecture and construction, which looks at integrating buildings with nature. It emphasizes perfect geometric patterns, symmetry and directional alignments. In recent years, it has gained popularity.

Several builders now market their constructions as 'vastu shastra compliant'.

But we did not want to go down that road. As engineers, we felt that vastu shastra was all about the right kind of construction and ventilation, and therefore, there was no need for us to alter anything.

If there was a jinx at all, it got broken soon enough. Our first tenant was industrialist K.K. Modi's daughter, Charu Modi, who leased a floor to set up an office for the Western International University.

After that, things began to move fast. Within no time, we were able to lease out all 60,000 square feet of space we had constructed. The market rate at that time was Rs. 27 per square foot per month; our average leasing price was Rs. 30 per square foot per month.

We had asked for one year's rent as our fees, which Choudhrie readily agreed to. Thus, we were able to earn over Rs. 2 crore from Golf View Corporate Towers. It was a small project, after all.

For Choudhrie, it turned out to be a sound investment. Apart from our fees, she had spent about Rs. 3 crore on refurbishing and repairing the building. Through the rents, she was able to recover her investment in less than three years. All income after that was profit for her.

We could meet our monthly expenses from the money we got from these two projects—Gurgaon One and Golf View Corporate Tower. We were happy that we did not need to dip into the equity capital to pay salaries, rent and power bills.

Our investors too became more confident in our abilities. As a part of the sanctioned project, there was an inbuilt floor-area ratio, called FAR in the Golf View Corporate Tower. In simple terms, we could construct more at the site.

Now that we had successfully delivered the project, we felt we should develop the rest of the FAR as well. Choudhrie readily agreed to our proposal. It is safe to assume that she was happy with the way we had done business with her.

One day, Rajiv Memani, the dapper India head of Ernst & Young, called to say that he was looking for office space of 1,00,000 square feet. I had known him from my days in the Great Eastern Shipping Company, and we had stayed in touch. And his father, Kashi Nath Memani, who was the earlier head of Ernst & Young, was acquainted with Col. Sodhi.

Through sheer hard work and high integrity, the senior Memani, a Marwari from Calcutta, rose through the ranks to head of one of the top professional services firms in the world. His is a truly inspirational story. After his retirement, the baton was passed on to his son, Rajiv Memani.

At that time, Ernst & Young's office in south Delhi was located in an unauthorized building and Memani wanted to move out of it as quickly as possible—an advisor to one of the top corporations in the world couldn't be seen violating the law himself.

We offered to construct 1,00,000 square feet of office space for him. We finished it in fifteen months flat and leased it out to the company for Rs. 45 per square foot per month. We collected six months of rent as our fees, which worked out to around Rs. 2.7 crore. Choudhrie couldn't have asked for anything more.

Word in the market was that we were the kind of people who did things the right way, didn't compromise on quality and delivered all projects well within the deadline. Even the top builders at that time could not make such claims.

I have often been asked about the role of ethics in business in general, and in the real estate sector in particular. Are contracts always handed out to the most deserving or are they influenced by other factors?

In my experience, I have seen both versions occur. While it is true that kickbacks are common in the corporate world, it is also true that reputation and capability are very important to any business. Trust is a very important factor in business. And you have to build it the hard way: through consistent hard work. You cannot let go of the benchmarks that you have set for yourself—a single slip-up could have an adverse impact on the business. You have to keep a constant vigil on your reputation in the market.

We had decided very early on that we would follow all the norms. The rules of the game were clearly laid out by Sheth on that fateful day in Mumbai many years ago. It was considered very experimental of us to brand ourselves as an ethical company, but I can say that the experiment yielded rich dividends for us.

Our shareholders seemed happy: they had no complaints. Our customers too were satisfied with what we had given them. Most importantly, our reputation in the market was improving with each project we undertook, as people realized that we were serious about keeping our promises and fulfilling our commitments. In a business where corruption was the norm and not the exception, this helped us stand out. And that is what helped us bag our next project.

In 2005, I happened to meet Sardar Daljit Singh Pannu through a bureaucrat friend. I was told that Pannu, who was then the Indian ambassador to Madagascar (he had also worked as a journalist and had been the ambassador to Ghana for eight years), has some twenty-four acres of land in Amritsar, and was trying to monetize it. My friend asked me if I could advise Pannu with regard to this.

I did not know what to expect: would he seek my advice to select one builder or would he ask me to make a pitch? With these questions buzzing in my head, I agreed to meet him. The next day, I met Pannu at Punjab Bhawan in New Delhi.

All the developers he had been talking to were in the lounge. Pannu had a very strong aura and looked an intellectual—I later came to know that he had even authored a book. It was difficult to not like him immediately.

At our first meeting, he told me about the land and how he wanted to make full use of its value. It would have been easy for me to just give him an opinion without thinking through the matter, but that would have been unfair on my part. I said that I would not be able to comment unless I saw the land and its location.

He agreed to show me the land. The next morning, I was on a train to Amritsar.

Amritsar is a populous city. Apart from being a popular pilgrimage destination, it is surrounded by huge tracts of agrarian land—it falls in the very fertile Majha area, often described as the wild west of Punjab. Many families from here have settled abroad and have done well for themselves. A lot of that money is sent back to the city and the villages around it. It is not uncommon to see lavish homes and enormous limousines in the midst of fields there.

Amritsar is also a hub for small and medium enterprises. It's very difficult not to get sucked into the city's bustle and energy. But as far as real estate was concerned, it was still virgin territory at that time.

Pannu's land was in the outskirts of the city, but was close enough to attract buyers. With the infrastructure development plans that had been drawn up for the city—an elevated corridor that would run very close to the Golden Temple—there was every reason to believe that this was prime property with tremendous possibilities. I was very impressed with what I saw.

When I met Pannu in Delhi next, he showed me what the various developers had offered him. They had all promised the moon to Pannu and sold him dreams that were not at all easy to achieve. I too could have matched their promises and then reneged on them at the time of delivery—it is not difficult in India where the variables are many.

Instead, I told him these were all great deals and I would not be able to offer him anything even close to it. That's the way we did business at Alpha G Corp.

I honestly thought this was the end of the matter. To my surprise, Pannu tore up the other proposals he had received and asked me if I had travelled to Madagascar or South Africa. When I replied in the negative, he requested I meet him in Madagascar as he was leaving the next day.

Pannu had a very mature head on his shoulders. It was clear that the fancy offers by the builders had not impressed him one bit.

I took the proposal to the Alpha G Corp board and apprised the members of the possibilities. They agreed there was a good deal of potential in the project and I was off to Madagascar.

I stayed in the only five-star hotel there, the Hilton. I was invited to the ambassador's house for breakfast and dinner. The treatment I received was nothing short of that reserved for a state guest.

The first day, after we finished dinner, Pannu gave me a list of questions that he had jotted down on a piece of paper. Nothing was discussed. Back in the hotel, I wrote the answers on another piece of paper and handed it over to him the next morning after breakfast. This was by far the most bizarre set of negotiations I had ever done.

That evening, after dinner, he gave me another set of questions. Once I returned to my room in the hotel, I wrote down my replies to his queries and gave it to him after breakfast the next morning. That was it. No conversation took place with regard to the matter.

Soon, I was on the flight back to India. To be frank, I was a little apprehensive. What would I tell my board—that all I had done was exchange two pieces of paper with Pannu? There was no conversation to report. I did know his concerns and had told him how we could address those, but Pannu had given me no indication of what he thought of my proposals.

But I need not have worried: as soon as I landed, I got a phone call from Pannu. 'Mr Sayal, prepare the agreement.'

However, there was a caveat. He said he liked our proposal but wanted Rs. 5 crore as payment upfront. That was big money for us. I told him we were a small company and didn't have that kind of money to pay him on such short notice. He replied, 'I am sending you the power of attorney, I don't know where you will get the money from, but just do it—after all, you are now the owner.'

When I recall those conversations, I now realize that he had made this demand only out of the great trust he had placed in us. Instead of rejecting his request outright, which would have meant losing out on a great opportunity, we decided to consider his request.

A solution came to us quickly. Now that we had the power of attorney, we said we could sell a part of the land which would help us raise Rs. 5 crore.

We spoke to IHHR, the company that ran Ananda in the Himalayas, the country's premier wellness retreat built on property owned by the erstwhile royal family of Garhwal.

Would they be interested in buying land for a hotel in Amritsar? It so happened that Ashok Khanna, who was running IHHR, had just launched a hotel brand called Ista. Looking at the potential the city offered, he was instantly interested.

This would be the first five-star hotel in Amritsar. Through the year, enough high-end visitors came to the city to keep the proposed hotel busy. We decided to sell 1.5 acres of the land to IHHR for Rs. 5 crore (Khanna, a grandson of Mohan Singh Oberoi, the legendary Indian hotelier, would later wind up the Ista chain. The Amritsar hotel is now owned by the Hyatt).

As soon as the deal was sealed, I called Pannu and told him that the money he had asked for was ready. He was relieved.

Pannu then told us that all the other builders he had spoken to had promised him an annual rental income of Rs. 5 crore. From us, he wanted a minimum guarantee of Rs. 2.5 crore for the first three years, perhaps because of the payment of Rs. 5 crore we had made upfront. it sounded like a reasonable request, and we agreed to it.

Soon, we signed a sixty–forty joint venture with him to develop the land. Out of the twenty-four acres, 1.5 acres had been sold to the hotel. In the first phase of development, we decided to build a mall on 10.5 acres of land.

We had constructed offices and residential buildings in the past. But a shopping mall was a whole new ball game for us. Though malls were the latest buzzword in real estate, there wasn't much expertise available to us. We were groping in the dark.

However, help came to us from an unexpected source.

Just when we had started work on the Amritsar project, Yahouda Naftalli, a global expert on malls, came to the city. He had a tie-up with the Choudhries for setting up malls under the brand BIG, but the project never really took off. We tapped into his expertise to design and plan the mall: the traffic management, the security angle, the visibility angle et cetera.

We had two or three fiery meetings with him and the architects who had, to their credit, created some 'funky' malls in the past. He trashed all our plans. He insisted on straight lines and visibility—all the retailers should be visible from the atrium. He also helped us locate the stores across the mall.

We learnt a lot from him. A mall is not just another construction: row after row of shops. It is designed scientifically and a lot of thought goes into the whole process. For instance, there are anchor stores, which see maximum footfall, and have to be visible from the entry. Convenience stores, from where visitors are likely to come out with the heaviest shopping bags, cannot be located too far from the exit. It is unwise to locate a food stall or restaurant between apparel stores. Open spaces are required at constant intervals, or the visitor may end up feeling claustrophobic.

Naftalli taught us all of this. His substantial inputs helped us complete the Amritsar mall in 2010. We were very sure we had a good thing going. But, unknown to us, trouble was brewing somewhere else.

Red tape has made India an unattractive place for doing business. In various 'ease of doing business' reports, India scores rather poorly, thanks to the various bureaucratic hurdles entrepreneurs are forced to face. Most of these hindrances are put up by the state and local administrations, as we were soon to find out.

We had built the Amritsar mall at a cost of Rs. 200 crore. When we applied for a completion certificate, we were confident it would be granted without any hassles because the entire construction had followed every rule in the book. There were no grounds for anyone to deny us the certificate.

The commissioner, however, wrote to us saying that while approving the mall, the authorities had forgotten to charge us a fee of Rs. 14 crore. We met him and told him that this was ridiculous. Everything was done according to the rules and regulations. Show us the law, we said, and we will pay the fee within twenty-four hours and get the certificate.

The commissioner said that the law for the fee had been recommended six or seven years ago to the state cabinet, but it had not yet been approved and notified by the state. This was outrageous. We met all the top administrators in the government, but these meetings proved fruitless. Unless we got the certificate, we could not hand over space in the mall to the retailers.

The whole construction threatened to become an idle asset. While the clock had started ticking for the debt repayment, there was no sign of any revenue coming in. First, the banks that had lent us money for the project began to chase us. Next, the buyers started calling us, anxious about the money they had put into the project.

We were under immense pressure. In fact, due to the delay, some retailers backed out of the agreement totally. As word got around that we hadn't got the clearance, people began questioning our credibility. This was damaging our brand equity, which we had worked so hard to build.

Finally, a whole year later, we got relief. We approached the High Court and the certificate was given to us under its direction.

But there was another twist in the tale. The court asked us to deposit the fee of Rs. 14 crore with the bank. We appealed against the order and the matter was heard by a bench. It asked the government to return the money to us, but asked us to furnish a bank guarantee of an equal amount. A bank guarantee for such a purpose comes only against 100 per cent margin money. In other words, instead of the government, we had to deposit Rs. 14 crore with the banks! The opportunity cost for us had not changed at all.

The delay cost us dearly. In the case of a completed project, there is a cost attached to each day's delay. In our case, the delay was a whole year—that added 10–15 per cent to our costs. The profitability of the project suffered due to the unnecessary delay. There is a need for the political leadership, and the bureaucracy, to be aware of business realities: It is unfair on their part to wreak havoc on investments.

While this example shows how bureaucrats, if they choose to, can make life difficult for a builder, the poisonous alliance between builders and bureaucrats too is an open secret. Even the top decision makers in the government get their cut from illegal deals with builders. All the violations in the sector can stop immediately if authorities decide to enforce the law properly.

But I do not foresee this happening any time soon. There is so much black money floating around in this sector that few can muster up the courage to overhaul the processes. 'It has repeatedly come to notice that builders, with officers of development authorities, flout every rule,' the Allahabad High Court noted in a recent judgement. 'The time has come when everyone should realize that the rule of law is not purchasable.'

In spite of all these problems, the mall was a success. It became the toniest shopping destination in Amritsar. Pannu was so charged with this success, he wanted us to launch the second phase of the project. By then, however, the market had begun to tank. We told Pannu that we would not be able to develop the mall with just 60 per cent equity stake and that we needed more. After discussing this with his sons and nephew, Pannu said we could get 3 per cent more equity for the second phase. We agreed to his proposition.

Unfortunately, Pannu was diagnosed with a life-threatening disease and passed away soon. But my relationship with the family continues. In fact, they don't take any decision related to the real estate sector without consulting me.

Meanwhile, the stock market was booming and real estate was the biggest beneficiary. The demand, investors were told, was galloping way ahead of the supply. Indians love buying houses for the social security they provide. The government had introduced income tax gains for those who took home loans. It was a sector that could stay on a high-growth curve forever.

Fantastic tales were spun around land banks, how these were assets waiting to be monetized. The investors lapped up these stories willingly. The herd mentality, so typical in a bullish market, was in full display.

One after another, the country's top builders listed through the IPO route. High valuations were there for the taking. A whole new generation of billionaires was born: K.P. Singh of DLF, the Chandra family of Unitech, among others. Their riches and lifestyle were the talk of the town. It looked like easy money.

Frankly, we too were tempted at Alpha G Corp to raise money through a public issue of funds. More money would have put us on a higher growth curve.

We took the proposal to our board of directors. We argued that we now had a strong track record and there were eminent people present on our board. We believed that the public issue of funds would be very successful. This was the time when even smaller builders managed to raise incredible amounts of money in the stock market.

But we ran into opposition in the form of our indomitable chairman, Ghanshyam Sheth. He argued that unless we could guarantee returns to the investors, nobody would buy our shares. It was, he added, morally incorrect to take money from unsuspecting investors in a buoyant market. He declined to approve our proposal.

'First show me three years of profits. Only when I see a great stream of income coming into the company, will I approve this move,' was all he said. According to him, if we followed his instructions, we could hope to be valued at Rs. 100 crore someday. He also made it clear that if we pushed for our case too hard, he would resign.

We had no option but to fall in line. We were yet to make profits consistently. After all, it was only just started getting projects and in real estate, it takes at least three years before revenue streams firm up.

In hindsight, Sheth's decision was the right one. A corporate entity cannot take a short-term view of the markets. In a bullish period, it is easy to sell anything. But markets are bound to turn around one day. Once that happens, the investors tend to get disillusioned. And they can be unforgiving. Any company that takes its investors for a ride cannot hope to raise money through them again. We too could have gone ahead and sold our shares without much effort at that time, but then there was a big question mark on our ability to deliver consistent long-term value to our investors. We were only thinking in the short-term then. And it was Sheth who opened our eyes to the long-term implications of our proposal.

However, at the same time, we needed growth capital. In its absence, we would continue to remain a small business entity for a long time. Some of us feared that we would soon get caught in a vicious cycle: our growth would continue to be low because of inadequate equity capital, and a public issue was not possible because of our lacklustre financial performance. This was a real dilemma, and none of us could see a way out of it.

Our prayers were answered soon when Morgan Stanley, the world's premier investment bank and fund manager, came into the picture in 2006.

Executives from the company had met Sheth in Mumbai; they were looking into the possibility of investing in his real estate business. However, he told them that he had just given up control of his real estate company to Anand Mahindra and his other ventures had not reached a scale where he would like to divest a part of his stake. Instead, he suggested that Morgan Stanley take a look at Alpha G Corp's financials.

Heeding his advice, they got in touch with us.

When we told its executives about our business model and the project we were working on, they were intrigued. After the company went through our books with a fine-toothed comb, Morgan Stanley said it wanted to buy into Alpha G Corp.

The initial seed capital of Rs. 15 crore had been put in by the original promoters of the company. By the time Morgan Stanley came into the picture, just Rs. 6 or 7 crore was left in the bank. And our venture's income streams had not yet stabilized. We asked the board what price we could quote to Morgan Stanley.

We were asked to seek professional advice. We met executives from Rothschild India in Mumbai. Their response was far from encouraging. They said we had no assets in our books and since our revenue streams were not clear, they didn't know how to value the company.

After a month of negotiating with these professionals, we were back to square one: Morgan Stanley was ready to invest in us, but we had no clue about how to value our company.

Every private equity fund has an investment committee, which approves or disapproves of any investment proposal. Without its go-ahead, the fund can make no investments. At that time, we were, in a sense of the word, like a start-up. We didn't have huge cash flows and a number of projects in the pipeline. But we had potential.

Morgan Stanley asked us to hand over our business projections in the form of a presentation. These projections would form the basis of our valuation. Unlike present times, when start-up valuations seem to defy all logic, we went through a proper process: every aspect of our future valuations was carefully detailed in the roadmap we prepared. Of course, we were conservative and realistic in our projections: we committed to nothing outlandish in our presentation.

We first submitted these projections and assumptions to the executives from Rothschild. They said we could ask for Rs. 400–450 crore for the whole company.

We thought this was nothing short of a miracle. In three years, a company formed with a seed capital of just Rs. 15 crore was now worth at least Rs. 400 crore. Our value had improved by over twenty-five times! This was beyond our wildest dreams.

Excited, we rushed back to the board with Rothschild's valuation. However, the board cautioned us to go slow. It was of the firm opinion that we first needed to build value within the company and then divest our stake. Our eagerness, first for a public issue and now for private equity, baffled the directors.

Companies were more conservative back then. These days, business ventures can raise private equity at a very early stage. Growth is more important for them than maturity. If you look at some of the top e-commerce companies today, you will realize that in many cases, the promoter has diluted his stake to below 26 per cent. They chase growth at all costs; in the process, if their stake comes down to such a level, they don't care.

Our shareholders were rather old-fashioned. In hindsight, I think they were comfortable with our steady pace of growth. The thought of growing too fast, too soon did not appeal to them. 'What's worrying you?' they asked us. 'Aren't you getting your salary on time?' They could not comprehend our urgent need to expand our business. There was no pressing need for money in the company, and they were reluctant to keep idle cash in the bank. They perhaps felt that if we waited longer, till the business became self-sustaining, our value in the market would increase manifold.

Now, when I look back at their arguments, I do see some merit in them. But back then, we felt very deflated by their attitude. The board wanted us to first finish those projects we had started work on, before moving on to newer ones.

It seemed to us that all our plans to increase our capital were jinxed. We called the executives in Morgan Stanley to tell them that the deal was off, but they refused to give up easily. Clearly, they had spotted potential in our business model.

Morgan Stanley's southeast Asia head, a Pakistani gentleman called Zain Fancy, came to meet us along with some representatives from its India division, Bharat Khanna and Anand Maduri. We met at the Hyatt, where I told them about our board's reservations. After hearing us out patiently, Fancy invited us to Hong Kong where he said he would show us a business model very similar to ours in which Morgan Stanley had invested.

Soon, Col. Sodhi, Sarin and I were on our way to Hong Kong. It is a great place for real estate development. At any given point in time, you can see old buildings being pulled down and new ones coming up in their place. Since space is limited, development has taken the vertical route in Hong Kong. To this day, it remains a favourite playground for Asia's rich and famous.

Fancy showed us the various projects that Morgan Stanley had invested in. After spending the whole day understanding how the company invested in various business models, he invited us over for dinner. After the dinner, he asked what would it take for us to divest stake in Alpha G Corp.

I told him that we may look at disinvestment, but not at a value below Rs. 1,500 crore. This was intended to throw him off our trail. When we reached our hotel, Fancy messaged me that the value I had mentioned was reasonable. We were elated, to put it mildly. It was late at night, but we were actually dancing on the streets!

It was the first time in India's history that a company had been valued so highly purely on the basis of the competence of its professionals. It was a wonderful feeling—we all felt like we were on top of the world.

Morgan Stanley's investment proposal came when we had just a handful of projects in hand and all of thirty-two people on our rolls. Unlike typical builders, we had no land bank to show in our books. The fees we collected helped us pay our salaries, the office rent and other administrative expenses.

Morgan Stanley had not seen a business model like ours in India. That it still chose to invest in us shows that the intangible assets of a company are just as important as its physical assets. The intellectual capital that resides in a company should never be undervalued. All we had at that time was a spotless reputation, project execution skills and the capacity to think out of the box. All of these factors had clearly shown in our business model.

And in the knowledge age we now live in, these are the aspects that will drive the valuation of an enterprise. Morgan Stanley, which was formed in 1935 and managed investments that ran into billions of dollars across the world, had faith in our business model and trusted our capability to deliver.

The Morgan Stanley offer was simply too good for the board to refuse. The firm bought a 20 per cent stake in Alpha G Corp for around Rs. 300 crore. Fresh shares were issued to Morgan Stanley, which meant the entire investment went into the company and not into anybody's pocket. We were all fine with this development. One thing was very clear to us: We were all committed to the company's growth; private gains could wait.

Apart from Alpha G Corp, the Choudhries owned another company called Grandeur Real Estate. It housed the land bank owned by the family, including some plots that were being developed by Alpha G Corp. When we got private equity from

Morgan Stanley at such huge value, the Choudhries perhaps felt that they could also unlock value in Grandeur too.

With our minimal assets we had managed to get valued at Rs. 1,500 crore, so they felt that with their land bank of over 200 acres they could get an even higher valuation. They began to scout for private equity with a value of Rs. 4,000 crore in mind. They even formed a team of professionals, from which we were excluded, to talk to some private equity funds.

But all their efforts came to naught. Eventually, we were called in to help them. We made the business plan and helped prepare the presentation. In spite working really hard for over two years towards this goal, they couldn't get the kind of valuation they had in mind. In fact, nobody was prepared to value them at more than Rs. 500 crore. It was abundantly clear to us that value is derived not just from physical assets but also from intellectual property that resides in the company. It is also important for the senior management to institutionalize that intellectual capital; otherwise, the whole enterprise collapses if one or two key people leave the organization.

One day, the Choudhries said that Citibank had approached them for a deal but they were keen to merge Grandeur and Alpha G Corp. The merger sounded reasonable to us. We had the intellectual capital but no physical assets—the merger would plug this gap. With these combined assets, we would be able to leverage our balance sheet and make it grow.

When the merger happened, Alpha G Corp was valued at Rs. 1,500 crore, which was the benchmark set by Morgan Stanley, and Grandeur was valued at around Rs. 500 crore. Since Grandeur was fully owned by the Choudhries, the merger increased their stake in Alpha G Corp, while the stakes of all the other shareholders went down. The company's balance sheet was strengthened with assets worth almost Rs. 700 crore. This was a huge gain for us.

In 2011, Morgan Stanley, after the financial meltdown of 2008, chose to step back and become a passive investor in the company. The subprime crisis had not left it untouched, and it had to work overtime to put its house in order. It continued to remain a dormant investor for the next few years.

We were under some pressure to go in for a public issue of shares in 2011, which would have given Morgan Stanley the opportunity to monetize its investment. But, by then, the stock market sentiment had begun to turn against the sector. The public issue never happened.

After the deal with Morgan Stanley and the merger with Grandeur, our owners, especially the Choudhries, gained immense confidence. They wanted to invest more money into assets. With this in mind, they asked us to be on the lookout for a township project.

In a sense, it seemed logical that Alpha G Corp work on a township. We had constructed a gated community, office projects and a mall; a township seemed to be the next logical step in our evolution.

One opportunity that came up was in Karnal, in Haryana. It is a centre for trade and commerce in the state and is a fairly prosperous place. However, it suffers from a distinct shortage of well-planned, urban space. We felt there could be a strong demand for good-quality housing here.

As per the rules, we needed twenty-five acres of land to get a licence to build a township. We started acquiring land for the Choudhrie family. It was decided that Alpha G Corp would build the township, based on our model of real estate asset management.

In this project, we were responsible for complete asset management: identification of the opportunity, acquiring the land, documentation, master planning, getting approvals and licences, execution, marketing and sales et cetera.

We were doing many of these things for the first time, but we believed that we could handle the challenge. The feedback from the market was positive. As a result, the twenty-five acres of the township grew to 100 acres and then to 200 acres, and today, that township is spread over 350 acres!

This was the first time that we were acquiring land directly for a project. And it just reiterated the basic lesson that land acquisition in this country is fraught with unnecessary intricacies.

Large chunks of the land faced big problems in the form of unclear title deeds. We, as a company with an overseas shareholder, could acquire land only where there was a master plan for development. Outside it, we couldn't buy even a square inch of land.

Most developers tend to buy land before they are covered by the master plan in order to save money. Once the area gets notified under the master plan, it sees a huge appreciation in its value. Needless to say, many developers often nudge the master plan along to ensure it is implemented. But we did not want to go down this road at all.

We stuck to our plan of only buying land in those areas that had already been notified under the master plan. As a result, we ended up paying more for the land. But this was the ethical way to go about it. We were buying the land from the farmers directly. For them, land isn't just any other commodity to trade; it means a lot more for them. Most farmers have lived off these lands for generations together. For them to turn their fields over to a builder requires a great leap of faith. There are also rifts and legal hassles within families, which makes acquisition all the more difficult for a builder.

Farmers often harbour the sentiment that the government acquires the land for very cheap and then sell it off at a much higher price. There is, therefore, great resentment against the government for acquiring land to sell to private players. The United Progressive Alliance government, in order to allay these concerns, brought in stringent consent clauses (land can be acquired only if 80 per cent farmers agree) and made it mandatory to conduct a social impact assessment before land is sold.

However, the industry was soon up in arms against these clauses, saying that this would strangle new projects. The National Democratic Alliance government tried to reduce the consent cutoff to 70 per cent and also increased the ambit of the purpose for which government can acquire land—the most notable of these new purposes was 'industrial corridors', which could have widened the scope for land acquisition hugely. Farmers, and their leaders, became more suspicious.

The government walks a fine line trying to balance the interests of the farmers and the industry.

In our case, land was being acquired directly by the builder—we had not involved the government at all—but we knew it was a sensitive matter, which needed to be handled with utmost care.

It is absolutely essential for a builder to have a proper relationship with the villagers. You can't fight the farmers because you have to do business with them. Many times, even after getting the money, they refuse to part with the land. This is why it is important to have experts on the ground with strong bonds with the local community, who can speak their language and quell their anxieties. Or else, the project is bound to get stuck.

For large projects, especially like townships, it is absolutely necessary that the land acquired forms a continuous chunk. If one or two landowners decide to play spoilsport, the entire project will be affected. To get everybody on board, it is important that you have someone who can be the face of your organization while dealing with the landowners.

If you have a limited budget for land acquisition, it is always best to begin by acquiring roads. A situation may arise where one or two landowners may choose to act difficult and you may end up owning land, but have no access to the nearest road. This can prove to be disastrous and derail the whole project. This also brings down the acquisition cost: If a landowner realizes that his plot of land is vital for the project, he will try to extract more and more money from you. Never underestimate their intelligence and street smarts.

We had appointed an aggregator to help us acquire the land. In the beginning, everything went smoothly. Only later that we learnt that he had registered small parcels of land under the names of his family members. These plots were strategically located, and their acquisition was very important for the successful execution of the project. If it came down to it, the company would have no option but to pay a premium amount for these plots.

We quickly recognized his intentions to make some easy money off us, and decided to terminate his services. It was not easy to let go of him, but we ensured nothing could hold up the project. We went on acquiring land on our own. By now we had a fair idea of how it was done and our credentials were well established with the landowners.

The size of these holdings varied from 1 acre to 15 acres. As long as the land was owned by one person, we faced no legal hassles. The problem came when the land was owned by the whole family. In such cases, we had to get all of them together and hammer out an agreement.

By the end of 2014, 200 acres of the township was already developed. The cost of land acquired varied from Rs. 10 lakh an acre to Rs. 2 crore an acre depending on the location. Alpha International City is located on the main highway to Karnal.

Meanwhile, we were approached by a United Kingdom-based fund that was keen to invest in the retail space and wanted us to scout for opportunities for it. This suited our real estate asset management model quite well—it would have also meant a good income for us.

We had heard of a government auction in Ahmedabad where the land could be developed into a mall. The Ahmedabad Urban Development Authority had put out an advertisement in the papers with regard to this. After consulting with the firm, we decided to participate in the bid on its behalf.

Four of us went to Ahmedabad: Pradipta Sen, the chief marketing officer, Ashish Sarin, chief financial officer, Mukul Kumar, the chief technical officer, and I.

The land was located near the Vastrapur Lake. However, the feedback we received about the location was extremely negative. People told us that Ahmedabad had more or less become some kind of a graveyard for the retail sector. Somehow they were unable to do well and were leaving the city. As a result, rentals were low. This, in turn, kept builders away from the retail space.

A recce of the city showed us that no serious player operated here because the city's infrastructure was not very robust—this was before Narendra Modi was elected as the chief minister of the state.

The picture was indeed dismal. But there were some positive factors too. The first, of course, was that Gujaratis are extremely industrious and prosperous people. It is not a stretch of the imagination to say that business is in their genes, which has translated into significant buying power. The biggest example of their success is their hold over the global diamond trade. They have turned Surat into the biggest centre in the world for the polishing of raw diamonds. They are also major players in the Antwerp diamond trade, the global hub for diamonds.

We also knew that the city was a prosperous one and people had the financial muscle to help retail trade grow. But there was no proper retail space in the city. The market was rife with potential. So there was a huge gap here which we could easily fill. With this in mind, we decided to participate in the auction.

If we won the land, we would have the first mover advantage, which is vital in real estate.

We met Surendra Kaka, chairman of the Ahmedabad Urban Development Authority, who was quite excited by our proposal. This reinforced our confidence. We were ready to bid up to Rs. 80 crore for the land, but managed to get it only for Rs. 52 crore!

With the knowledge we gained from our association with Naftalli and our experience of working on the Amritsar mall, Alpha One, our mall in Ahmedabad, was a resounding success. In no time, all the space was rented out.

Working on the Amritsar and Ahmedabad projects drove home the realization that a mall is not just real estate development—it is a business that takes its own time to bear fruit, much like hotels. And it ought to be undertaken only by those people with really deep pockets because it could face losses for quite a few years.

It takes almost three to five years for a mall to stabilize. Then there are the retailers: Some want to move out because they may have made incorrect projections, while others may want to reduce the floor space.

This was a serious problem for us at Alpha G Corp. We were relatively undercapitalized. This meant that we lacked the wherewithal to hold on to a mall for long. That's why our original idea was to build the mall, sell the space as quickly as possible and book our profits. But that was just a short-term view of the business, and not really the right one.

Executives at Morgan Stanley told us that malls would never be successful if the builder sells off the space. It will be successful only if the builder owns the space and gives it to retailers on lease.

The logic was simple yet elegant. Malls provide an experience. The moment a developer sells the space off, he loses all control over creating that experience.

The biggest problem in India now is that a majority of the mall developers choose to sell the space outright. When malls first started coming up, many of the developers were told that they should only lease out the space. But they lacked the capacity to hold on to the mall until the profits stabilized. It is an asset heavy business.

By now, our portfolio boasted of a variety of projects: residential as well as commercial. Through word of mouth, people had come to know of us. Most important, people spoke well of us.

As a result, we started getting a lot of offers for joint ventures. But we decided to be discerning about the kind of projects we chose.

We chose our projects very carefully. Two of these were located in Amritsar: the first one was the 150-acre Model Industrial Park, which was a joint venture with a local developer, and the next was the Alpha International City at Amritsar—a residential project—in association with Veer Developers. Our job was to build the infrastructure and do the landscaping.

We were also approached by a Chennai-based developer called H.S. Ratha, who had his roots in Punjab, for another residential project. He had around 100 acres of land in Mohali, the area that has come to be known as New Chandigarh, and signed us on for the job. Again, we came in as the real estate asset managers.

In any business, it is important to know when to draw the line on expansion. Growth has to be in sync with the managerial bandwidth. If a company takes more work than what it is capable of managing efficiently, the results are often disastrous.

I remember in the 1990s—in the years that followed economic liberalization, there was easy money floating around and businessmen used the opportunity to diversify recklessly into unrelated areas. In most cases, these investments ended in pain and grief. That's because they did not have the wherewithal to manage so many businesses at once. As a result, many of them saw a serious erosion in their brand equity, which they are yet to regain.

We too could have leveraged our goodwill to launch a whole range of projects. But that would have been unfair to our partners and our customers. We were, in spite of our successes, still a small company, and didn't want to stretch ourselves too thin. The managerial bandwidth of any enterprise is finite; it has to be used judiciously.

Meanwhile, another factor soon came into play: the economic slowdown. Many reasons have been attributed to this. One, the runaway inflation, especially the sharp rise in food prices, which caused the Reserve Bank of India to raise interest rates. This, in turn, is believed to have choked investments as well as consumer spending across categories, real estate included.

The food inflation was caused by the serious increase in the support prices of staple foods like wheat and rice. It is widely acknowledged that food inflation affects the poor the most, because they spend a larger part of their income on staples, and that's why it became necessary for the Reserve Bank of India to follow a tighter monetary policy.

The other factor was the retrospective taxation introduced by Pranab Mukherjee when he was the Union finance minister in his budget for 2012–13. That, many commentators said, had scared away all foreign investors and brought India's economy to a near halt.

Whatever be the reason, it was soon evident that the glory days of the real estate sector would soon be over. A more realistic phase would now begin.

This affected Alpha G Corp too. We started selling the township at Amritsar in 2011, and it took us almost three years to sell it fully. There were close to 1000 plots in the 100 acres.

In 2013, we started selling the industrial park in Amritsar. Sales were slow right from the beginning because it was a new concept for that market. There were seven to eight plots in an acre. Of course, the economic slowdown too had an impact on the project.

But the intrinsic worth of the industrial park remained intact. The new generation of entrepreneurs in Amritsar wanted better infrastructure and were reluctant to operate out of the cramped environs within the city. About 200 plots were sold by the end of 2014, which is about 20 per cent of the total space.

In the midst of the slowdown, we launched another residential project in Gurgaon. It was in Sector 84; so we called it Gurgaon One Sector 84. The land was owned by Magnum International, which was again controlled by the Choudhrie family.

We had 12 acres of contiguous land on which we planned to build 660 dwelling units. The apartments were smaller in size, when compared to Gurgaon One in Sector 22, because here we were catering to the middle-income market. The apartment sizes varied from 1200 to 3000 square feet.

In the slowdown, it was our brand equity that helped us sell the project. We had made a niche space for ourselves by ensuring all our promises to the investors were met. When we launched the project, the rate was Rs. 3000 a square foot. While the market elsewhere turned soft, we raised the prices first to Rs. 4000 a square foot and then to Rs. 5500 a square foot. Sales were brisk.

6

An Anonymous Offer

The financial meltdown of 2008 had been in the making for quite some time. It all started in the United States where banks were loaning money freely to people to buy houses. The real estate market there went into a bullish phase. Everybody seemed to be investing in the sector.

Like it happens in any bullish run, the due diligence norms were overlooked. Nobody seemed to be prepared to believe that one day the party would end. It later came to light that people had raised multiple loans on the same assets: houses were mortgaged to more than one lender. It was easy money and everybody wanted a share of it.

But the market could not sustain this unprecedented rise. When the bubble burst and prices went into decline, the banks realized that the assets they held as collateral were grossly inadequate and could not cover their loans. In other words, if they took control of the assets they had lent against and sold them, they would still incur a loss.

This precipitated the subprime crisis. Bank after bank collapsed. Lehman Brothers was the first to go under. The real estate market in the United States went into a tailspin because of the crisis. Nobody wanted to be a part of it. In very little time, the sector went from boom to bust.

For a while, it seemed as though India too would be affected by the crisis, but luckily the country escaped the worst of it. That's because Indian banks had almost zero exposure to subprime loans. Moreover, Indians are conservative borrowers. There is a certain stigma associated to defaulting on loans. While in the United States there is no great shame associated to losing a house due to non-payment of loans, an Indian takes it seriously—he tries his best to avoid such a situation.

Given the breakneck speed at which the real estate sector had grown in India over the last few years, there was some fear that the sector would collapse here too. However, there was only one temporary setback, which resulted in some soul searching and stock taking—but the sector did not face any serious trouble.

Once it was clear that the conditions that led to the subprime crisis in the United States did not exist in India, the sentiment perked up again. Unlike the situation in the West, Indians had started buying homes and commercial property by the middle of 2009 again.

The country's economy too was able to absorb the shock of the crisis quickly. India's gross domestic product growth fell from 9.3 per cent in 2007–08 to 6.8 per cent in 2008–09, but rose to 8 per cent in 2009–10 and 8.5 per cent in 2010-11.

Even though the crisis didn't affect India directly, it wasn't as if the country was totally immune to the external shocks. It was, after all, the biggest jolt to the global economy after the Great Depression of the 1920s.

The stock market suffered significant reverses due to the global crisis. As investment banks incurred losses on their home ground, they dumped their stocks in emerging markets like India to shore up their financial performance. And as investors withdrew from India, the various stock indices began falling sharply. There is always a wealth effect precipitated by such a crash—people begin to think they have become poorer and started to postpone all discretionary purchases.

However, the real estate sector remained largely unaffected by the fall in the stock market. As real estate prices remained steady, people concluded that it was safe to invest in this sector. It still offered 15 to 20 per cent annual appreciation, plus another 3 per cent as rental income, which was better than other traditional assets like stocks, fixed deposits and the bullion.

Developers began working at a frenetic pace again. Unfortunately, most of them overlooked the fact that every sector must go through business cycles. In the bullish phase of the market, everybody believed the demand for real estate would never fall in India.

There were several projections with regard to urbanization and migration that made people believe that supply would always stay short of the demand for several decades to come. In other words, the popular belief was that real estate would remain a sellers' market—where builders could dictate terms to the buyers.

When the market is on the upswing, it is remarkable how nobody wants to believe that it could all turn south one day. Those who as much as utter a word of caution are shouted down as alarmists or party poopers. In times of mass euphoria, sanity is usually the first casualty.

And then, one day, the unthinkable happened. By 2011, we could sense that the market was starting to stagnate. Prices had stopped escalating. In the last few years, the market had seen prices rise sharply—so much so that houses were becoming out of reach for many buyers. We sensed that people had stopped purchasing real estate, and were, instead, waiting for the prices to fall. These were the first warning signs that things were going to take a turn for the worse.

And soon enough, the downturn began. Demand started to peter out. Prices didn't come down, though most markets saw some correction. Builders began to talk, first in hushed tones and then quite openly, about how it was getting more and more difficult to sell projects. In some quarters, outrageous offers were being made: a free car with each flat for instance.

With the Reserve Bank of India raising interest rates, home loans had become expensive. The slowdown, induced by the tight monetary policy, tore into corporate earnings. Increments were postponed. Many companies were forced to downsize their operations. As the fears of unemployment multiplied, people began putting off discretionary purchases.

By 2014, the market had come to a near standstill. There were no buyers. Everybody knew that the supply had galloped ahead of the demand, and the builders were now saddled with unsold stock. People started to feel that this may not be the right time to buy. They thought that by waiting a little longer, they could get a better price.

Around Diwali that year, I met with some builders who had mounted high-decibel advertising campaigns in the hope of finding buyers. But they all said the inauspicious period that precedes Diwali had continued during the festival of lights. All the money they had invested in the promotion of their projects had come to naught. They had zero returns on their investment.

Housing finance companies were haunted by the risk of default. There were many reasons for this. One, many people had bought multiple houses as an investment. They now realized that the investment had turned sour. While there was little yield, in terms of rental income and capital appreciation, the higher interest rate had increased their liability. Two, the slowdown had eaten into their capacity to repay bank loans.

The fact is, the bubble was in the making for some time now—the supply was far in excess of what genuine home buyers wanted. When interest rates were low, housing finance was booming. When the demand died down, there emerged a serious glut in the market.

Bech ke pachhtao, or sell first and then regret it, used to be a common refrain in the industry. In a market on the upswing, real estate developers usually adopt the policy of hoarding property in the hope of selling at better prices later.

This works well when the market is buoyant, but fails when prices go into a decline. The builders then need to book losses in their inventories—something businessmen loathe doing. It works in another way too: as the value of the builder's assets decline, because of the fall in prices, his ability to leverage it against debt also reduces.

And this is precisely what happened. Once the demand came to a grinding halt, there was a rapid pile-up of unsold inventory. Large sums of money—contributed by buyers, investors, builders and banks—got stuck in the sector.

Of course, several developers had overbuilt during this period, never anticipating that the demand would fizzle out.

Noida is a case in point of how the sordid drama played out. The builders there constructed at least half-a-dozen condominiums. Much of the stock remained unsold, which meant the builders' cash flows had more or less dried up. As a result, almost all the projects were running late.

This eroded the builders' credibility. Buyers were starting to get angry as they had no idea when they would get possession of their flats. Those who had purchased houses purely for investment purposes were also stuck. The secondary real estate market simply vanished.

The Uttar Pradesh government also played a big role in causing this crisis. The state government had in 2008, when the Bahujan Samaj Party was in power, allowed builders to pay only 10 per cent of the land cost upfront—the rest could be paid in instalments over several years, though with an interest.

The idea behind the rule was to give a boost to the local economy. However, it ended up having a totally different consequence: in one stroke, the entry barriers had all come down. It became easy for a lot of people to launch housing projects.

Many non-serious builders entered the Noida market at that time. As a result, by 2013 there was a huge oversupply in the market. As the real estate business is built on turning money around, the slowdown wreaked havoc on their finances.

Broker commissions were as high as 12 per cent from the 4 per cent it was two years ago. Many builders engaged celebrities to endorse their projects. One builder even offered a flat free with the purchase of a penthouse! All of these were clearly the ominous signs of an impending crisis.

If the situation in Noida was bad, it was worse in Greater Noida. The township was supposed to house several companies and factories, and it was assumed that the people who worked here would require housing close-by. But that did not happen.

The industrial slowdown that began in 2009 drove away all potential investors. Many organizations at that time preferred to invest in Uttarakhand and Himachal Pradesh, which offered substantial fiscal incentives. Some companies chose to expand in more investor-friendly states. Honda, for example, located its second car factory in Rajasthan.

However, builders continued to construct the houses and flats. As a result, Greater Noida began to resemble a ghost town: tall buildings and luxurious houses everywhere, but not a soul inside. It was clear that it would take several years for the builders to get rid of their inventories. The annual rental income came crashing down to 0.5 per cent of the capital cost! Capital appreciation became zero, if not negative.

Now and then, the developers tried to create some excitement in the market but nothing seemed to help. First, the government gave its go-ahead to extend the Delhi Metro to Greater Noida. The second was the proposal for an international airport just ahead of Greater Noida. The proposal had first been moved when Mayawati was the chief minister of Uttar Pradesh. It then went into cold storage because such an airport, it was feared, would impact the fortunes of the GMR-led Delhi International Airport. In late 2014, the proposal was brought out of cold storage, most likely at the behest of the developers. But it failed to generate any buzz in the market.

The situation across the country was no different. In June 2012, a report in *Mint*, quoting data supplied by PropEquity Analytics, said that sales had tumbled as much as 15 per cent in key markets of the country like Delhi–NCR and the Mumbai Metropolitan Region.

The PropEquity analysis predicted that prices could be corrected by 5 to 20 per cent in these two markets. The *Mint* report told buyers they could expect more freebies and easier payment options.

But as the days passed, the situation only got worse. A report that appeared in *Business Standard* in September 2013 said that the inventories of the nineteen real estate companies that were a part of the BSE 500 index had climbed from Rs. 36,686 crore in 2008–09 to Rs. 57,807 crore in 2012–13.

The builders with the biggest inventory at the end of 2012–13 were DLF (Rs. 17,465 crore), followed by HDIL (Rs. 12,043 crore), IndiaBulls (Rs. 5,110 crore), Unitech (Rs. 4,402 crore) and

Omaxe (Rs. 3,533 crore). The report said that it would take the builders at least two years to get rid of the inventory. The optimal level of inventory in real estate is eight to ten months. Anything above that is a strain on the resources. .

There is a strong correlation between inventory and borrowings. That's why the combined borrowings of the nineteen companies at the end of 2012–13 were to the tune of Rs. 51,000 crore, according to the report. At 12 per cent interest, it would cost the builders over Rs. 1,500 crore every quarter.

The situation went from bad to worse. According to data provided by Liases Foras and quoted in a report in *Business Standard* in November 2014, Delhi and its suburbs were sitting on inventory of eighty-three months at the end of September 2014. In Mumbai as well as Chennai, the inventory would take fifty months to clear. In Bangalore, it was forty-one months; and in Hyderabad, thirty-eight months.

Because of the sheer volume of the unsold inventory, even global investors lost their appetite. Foreign direct investment in construction, according to the *Business Standard* report, plummeted from $3.1 billion in 2011–12 to $1.3 billion in 2012–13 and then dipped to $1.2 billion in 2013-14. During the first four months of 2014–15, foreign direct investment in this sector was just $446 million.

In October 2014, the National Democratic Alliance government led by Narendra Modi, in an attempt to revive the sector, relaxed the norms for foreign direct investment in the real estate.

Among other things, the minimum built-up area required for foreign investment was slashed from 50,000 to 20,000 square metres, and the project size was halved to $5 million. Under the rules, 100 per cent foreign investment was allowed in real estate projects.

However, with so much unsold inventory left, it was not clear how these changes would help the sector. And in the months that followed, foreign investors did choose to stay away from India.

This problem of a high inventory of unsold goods spread from residential to commercial real estate as well.

Another report that appeared in *Business Standard* in November 2014, quoting figures provided by Jones Lang Lasalle, showed that absorption of retail space in malls fell from 10.7 million square feet in 2011 to 4.5 million square feet in 2012. It rose to 5.1 million square feet in 2013 before slumping to 2.2 million square feet in 2014. The report said that at least two malls in Mumbai were converted into office complexes, while four in Delhi were staring at imminent closure. Prozone, a company promoted by apparel maker Provogue and Capital Shopping Centres, scaled down its plans from six malls to three, according to the report.

The reasons for this could be the high price of land, which is totally out of sync with purchasing power, the slowdown in the economy and the rise of e-commerce—its share in the $600-billion retail pie is projected to swell from $4 billion in 2014 to $22 billion in 2018.

According to one analysis, of the 300 or so operational malls in the country, only around twenty were doing well. One mall in Noida had to engage a consultant to find ways to beat the challenge posed by e-commerce retailers. The ease of shopping online, plus the uniquely Indian features like cash on delivery and free returns, had taken the punch out of brick-and-mortar retail stores.

By the middle of 2014, it was not uncommon to find malls empty, even on public holidays and festivals.

Of course, it was the investors who got the short end of the stick. Thanks to the inordinately long delays that afflicted the projects, many began to find it tough to pay the instalments on their home loans.

According to a report *The Indian Express* in November 2014, non-performing assets in the home loan portfolio of state-owned banks jumped by almost Rs. 1,000 crore during the first six months of 2014–15, pointing to rising stress in the system.

As a proportion of total home loan assets, NPAs increased from 1.38 per cent to 1.54 per cent at the end of September 2014. The situation was not alarming, but it was hard to deny that the system was under pressure.

Many builders who had taken loans from banks found themselves in a tight spot. As sales came to a standstill, their internal cash generation dried up and they found it difficult to rustle up the money to meet the quarterly interest payments.

I used to know a private lender who worked with developers. In late 2014, he told me that most developers who had borrowed from the banks at 12 to 13 per cent interest were unable to repay the money. So, to avoid defaulting on loans, they started to approach the non-bank finance companies, or NBFCs, who were lending at 18 to 20 per cent. In a sense, these developers had entered a vicious cycle: they needed to borrow more money in order to repay earlier debts. With sales grinding to a halt, they had to borrow money to complete their ongoing projects.

And the cycle just continued. Those defaulting with the NBFCs then went to private lenders for money who charged up to 35 per cent interest. With such costs, which business could claim to be successful?

To look at it from a different perspective, why were private lenders ready to take such a high-risk exposure when they knew the cash flows of the developers had dried up?

I asked one lender about this and he said that they were lending money against assets they wanted to buy. His logic was quite straightforward: once the builder defaults, he has no option but to sell the asset, and this gives them the leverage to buy the asset at a discount—after all, it is wise to pick up good assets in any distress sale.

He said he did not run the risk of not getting his money back. It struck me that he was just acquiring real estate assets through this route.

Even the investments made by private equity funds were no longer vanilla deals: most of these were structured deals with assurances of returns of 18 to 22 per cent.

You can well imagine what all this was leading to. It was clear to everyone that it was just a matter of time before the real estate bubble burst. Until the end of 2014, banks were okay with lending out money because the developers, either through NBFCs or private lenders, were still able to repay them.

But these developers could not keep borrowing from one source or the other. The day the funds of NBFCs and the private lenders runs out, banks would have been the worst affected. The market would have plunged into chaos.

Interest rates for real estate were always higher than the other sectors because of the greater risk factor involved here. Hence, if a bank was lending money to others at 10 per cent, builders would be charged around 12 per cent interest.

Such high costs of funds have always had a negative impact on the business of most builders. This has impaired the creditworthiness of the sector, and affected its access to resources.

Banks started tightening the noose after they realized that the builders had inflated the value of the assets they had given as collateral. This caused a serious mismatch of assets and liabilities for many banks. This was when the Reserve Bank of India stepped in, and began to caution banks against lending money to developers.

The banks also felt that some builders may have diverted the funds to other causes. A lot of these loans were then restructured.

Slowly, but very surely, the stock market too turned against the real estate sector. The unsold inventories and enormous amounts of debt scared investors away. Consumer activism and the various land scams only made matters worse.

At one point in time, there was a lot of euphoria about the primary market. Many builders leveraged it to raise money at high valuations. Even those with half-baked business models and a modest reputation in the market were quick to jump on the bandwagon. By 2014, most of them were trading at historical lows.

So much so, many could have actively looked at delisting their company from the markets—such was the fall in their share prices. The stock market became a no-go area for developers. And it was clear that the situation was unlikely to improve any time soon. I couldn't visualize any developer doing a public issue of shares in the near future, though I felt corporations in the real estate sector would do better because of the trust and confidence that the buyers have in them.

The ugly truth about the sector finally spilled out in July 2015.

A report by Ambit highlighted the impact of the real estate meltdown. Taking note of falling prices and the significant dip in transactions, it cited several factors for the slowdown: the banks stopped lending to builders, the shift to direct benefit transfers, which has reduced the illegal diversion of subsidies, the pile-up of unsold inventory, the severe Black Money Bill, the 8 per cent gap between rental yields and bank base rates, and the unrealistic ready-reckoner rates fixed by many states.

As real estate contributes half of the country's capital formation and 30 per cent of its jobs, this made Ambit scale down its growth projection for 2015–16 from 7.8 per cent to 7 per cent.

It then went on to recommend to its clients that they should sell some stocks in sectors related to real estate: cement, paints and banks.

For us in the industry, it was clear by the end of 2014 that the conventional model of real estate development had run its course. The problem was cash flows: there were no new sales happening, equity markets had turned cold and it was hard to get loans.

Alpha G Corp followed an asset-light model, and therefore, the dependence on loans was very limited. This meant that the high interest charged by lenders did not strangle our cash flows. But it had a flip side too: the limited access to capital often came in our way of growth.

There were times that we were approached by landowners with large land banks for development. But we had to turn down many of these offers because we did not have the resources—even though we didn't have to pay for the land, there were several other expenses to be taken care of.

You can't start construction on an empty patch of land right away. A licence fee needs to be paid first followed by external development charges, a government fee, infrastructure development charges, a scrutiny fee, conversion charges, and all the other charges the government levies on land.

These charges are pretty steep: they can be as high as Rs. 4-5 crore per acre in Gurgaon. So, if it's a 50-acre land parcel, you need Rs. 240–250 crore in your pocket before you can even think of starting work on the project. Since we didn't have this kind of money, we had to let go of many good opportunities. It was a very frustrating time and the strain was starting to show. We did raise debts from the banks, but it was mainly on the assets that we owned—either on our own or with our partners.

Our business model had fetched us terrific valuation a few years ago but there was no way we could leverage it to raise money. Due to our financial discipline, because of which our default rate was zero, bank loans were never really a problem for us. Even when other builders said that the banks were acting tough, we didn't face any particular problem.

However, the negative investor sentiment affected us too. We had gone for private equity after it was decided that we wouldn't tap the stock market. The very fact that a private equity fund had become a shareholder in our organization meant that one day we would have to give them an exit. This would either be through a secondary sale or most probably through an IPO. Internally, the understanding was that it would be latter. The question was not how, but when.

When Morgan Stanley had invested money in Alpha G Corp, we set a time frame of five years for listing the company on the stock market through a public issue. That would have given Morgan Stanley a route to monetize its investment in us and given the company capital to grow.

In real estate, projects have a long gestation period; so we thought we would have some regular income in some time—all our projects would be up and running. The idea was that when we go to the market, we should have a stable business and the wherewithal to work on upscale projects.

When the sector was on the upswing, we expected a valuation that was thirty to forty times of our earnings. But when we discussed the matter internally, we felt we might not be in a position to sustain such a high investment.

We did not want to make any false commitments in the market for short-term gains. So we decided to build value in the company first.

Any other developer at that time, with the kind of income streams we had opened, would have gone for a public issue of shares. But we had stronger ethics.

However, by the time our business had stabilized, the market had started to take a dim view of real estate. The window of opportunity had closed.

Once the market had turned adverse, our IPO plan became dormant. The market lost all appetite for real estate paper. All the top builders lost substantial value and controversies began to dog the sector.

Had we depended solely on the stock market for funds, we would have been in serious trouble. Thankfully, we were able to build a regular stream of income from our rented assets. These were projects that took four to five years to stabilize, like the malls in Amritsar and Ahmedabad, but they gave us a regular income.

About 80–85 per cent of the Amritsar mall had been leased out. But the one in Ahmedabad was close to 100 per cent occupancy. A regular income from these assets helped us pay back our debt and meet our regular expenses. So our credit rating was much higher than others.

However, this was also the time when retailers started pressuring malls to reduce the rent. Where negotiations failed, retailers just shut their stores and cut their losses. Many retailers moved from fixed rents to revenue share. As they threatened to move out if their demands were not accepted, the mall owners were left with no option but to decrease rents.

Fortunately, in our malls the rents were not very high. Those who had charged higher rents had to face financial losses.

This is not to say we didn't face problems at all. Many of the retailers who had leased out space realized that they had over-committed. Clearly, the business projections they had made had gone awry. The slowdown curtailed discretionary purchases of households. E-retail had only made matters worse. We had to pay the price for their erroneous projections.

Why weren't the retailers able to anticipate their business correctly? One often feels that executives overestimate the market potential while projecting the figures to their bosses in order to get bigger budget allocations. This makes them feel important and powerful.

In a sense, this is what also happens with stock options—the companies often create a vested interest amongst employees to inflate the financial performance of a company, so that the value of the stocks remains high.

Several minor and major scams perpetrated by employees with stock options have come to light over the years, the biggest being Enron—the US-based power major—which perished under the weight of the scandal many years ago.

There has to be a system of rewards and punishments for those executives who prepare business projections. While those who predict the forecasts correctly should be rewarded, those who make outlandish projections should be taken to task. There are too many instances of shareholders' value getting eroded through erroneous projections, but seldom does one hear of anybody in the company held accountable for this.

Highly paid consultants too are often guilty of making incorrect business projections.

I know of a telecom service provider which had appointed a highly respected consultancy to study the potential for mobile telephony in Delhi in 1994. After huffing and puffing for a while, the consultancy said that the company could hope to find 5,000 customers in the city! It was worse than a joke—today, almost everyone in Delhi, a city of several million people, owns a mobile phone.

In the early 1990s, an overseas footwear company drew an estimate of the Indian market by looking at the number of cars on the roads. Every car owner was a potential buyer for its high-end products.

The company did not account for the simple fact that almost all Indians buy cars in instalments and many drive around in the cars given to them by their employers. This led to a gross overestimation of the market potential. The company realized its mistake quickly and had to do some serious price correction in order to enter the market.

It was the same problem with retailers: overenthusiastic consultants and employees had sold them bizarre projections. And when the mistake was realized, they were left with no option but to resort to course-correcting measures.

Once the boom years ended, it was clear to us that there was no science behind the sizing of stores. Initially, everybody thought of utilizing bigger spaces as it would give them high visibility, help them negotiate better rents and open up revenue streams like restaurants and stores.

Hypercity wanted to set up a store in Amritsar, which would be spread over 1,40,000 square feet. Shoppers Stop also wanted 80,000 square feet in the mall. We were initially very excited by their enthusiasm. Together, these two retailers, both owned by the Raheja Group, occupied nearly 40 per cent of the total space of the mall.

But it soon became clear to us that the returns were nowhere close to what they had assumed. We had thought that these were the country's retail gurus who would teach us a trick or two about the business. But it was obvious that they were groping in the dark and had grossly miscalculated.

The result was that they stopped paying us rent. When we asked them for the money, they said the rent had become unaffordable.

This put us in a quandary. Obviously, if they were not making money, how would they be able to pay us rent? At the same time, they were the anchor tenants of the mall; if they packed their bags and left, it would have earned the mall a bad name—buyers would have been confused and the whole place would have looked like a ghost town.

Another reason we did not want them to leave was that it would have taken us a lot of time to find another set of anchor tenants.

After much deliberation, it was decided that the stores should downsize. Thus, the Hypercity unit was reduced from 1,40,000 square feet to 60,000 square feet and the Shoppers Stop store was reduced by half. We resisted their pressure to slash the rent but agreed to move to a revenue share model.

This worked, just like it had worked in the telecom sector. As long as the government extracted a fixed rent from the mobile phone companies, all of them were bleeding; the moment the government moved to a revenue share model, all of them started making profits.

This was a great learning experience for us. We had to start renting out the space vacated by the two retailers in a piecemeal manner. Finally, we had tenants on fixed rent, minimum guaranteed rent as well as those who shared revenue with us.

The fact that just one group leased out 40 per cent space in the mall was a tactical error on our part. It had exposed us to great risk. That's why in Ahmedabad, where our mall was much bigger at over 7,00,000 square feet, we decided to have several anchor tenants: Home Store, Shoppers Stop, Lifestyle and Reliance Trends. We had realized that we cannot be held to ransom by any one of them—our risks were adequately covered.

Most of the space was given out on fixed rentals and a revenue share with a minimum guarantee. There were very few stores on just a revenue share model.

Both the malls started meeting their operating expenses by 2014, but the one in Amritsar had some vacancy. It also saw the space changing several hands as the city has a huge mobile population. In Ahmedabad, as the population is more static, we did not face this issue.

However, we weren't so lucky with our township project in Karnal, where the unsold inventory was to the tune of Rs. 500 crore. In the 350 acres of the township, the company had 100-plus acres that had not even been licensed by the end of 2014.

Our aim was to complete all the work that we had started. In hindsight, we probably overestimated the demand in Karnal. When we had launched the township, we had thought that people from the surrounding areas would quickly buy space in the project.

There was plenty of purchasing power in the area, but many buyers wanted to pay in cash, which went against our principles. Therefore, sales remained sluggish and well below our projections.

In September 2013, I lost my father. It was a huge personal blow for me. Professionally too, I was not very happy and had started to feel that my time at Alpha G Corp had run its course. I was not actively looking out for another job, but had decided to consider the offers that came my way.

Several major developers had got in touch with me and had made me offers; but I had turned all of them down. Head-hunters would call me every three months or so with fresh offers. Now, I decided to re-evaluate my options. There were a few reasons for it.

Real estate is a highly capital-intensive business. And I knew that Alpha G Corp was undercapitalized. With banks reluctant to loan large sums of money and equity markets, including private funds, becoming cold to real estate, I had a distinct feeling that the drought of funds would not end any time soon.

This was beginning to show on the company's growth chart. It is a basic tenet of management that people stay motivated only when the organization can grow. In its absence, frustration starts to set in. That leads to attrition and the loss of human resource capital.

We had started the company on an asset management model. This was a fee-based business and did not require a large capital base. The fee we got from managing assets was supposed to help sustain us. But that wasn't enough for us to go after more projects. We had made the company a model for others to follow in terms of project execution and delivery, and ethical practices. But Alpha G Corp was starved of capital, which meant the growth prospects weren't bright—neither for the company nor for the senior leadership team.

The investment by Morgan Stanley had brought Rs. 300 crore into the company, but the funds were locked in the two malls in Amritsar and Ahmedabad. Our original plan was to sell space and exit the malls, which would have helped us recover the money. But, as per Morgan Stanley's advice, we decided to look for rental income instead.

Morgan Stanley had indicated that it would bring in more growth capital in the future. But the plan fell through after the 2008 liquidity crisis.

There was some negative publicity too. When Morgan Stanley had valued us at Rs. 1,500 crore, or 120 times of our paid-up capital, a lot of people had said that the predictions were all up in the air because we had no physical assets. That was true, though we did have sufficient intellectual capital—an intangible asset. By the time we managed to get some physical assets on our books, the stock market had lost all appetite for real estate paper.

We were in a bind.

I broached this subject frequently with the principal promoters of the company, the Sheth and Choudhrie families. But they seemed reluctant to expand the equity capital of the company. One reason for this could be the fact that both of them had other interests in real estate as well. They had together floated two more companies: G Corp (South) and G Corp (West). They now wanted to consolidate their business and merge these two companies with Alpha G Corp.

A merger always creates some anxiety amongst senior executives. I had sensed it earlier when Gesco Corporation was taken over by Anand Mahindra. I had expressed my fears to the shareholders, who assured me that I had nothing to lose. In fact, they promised to make me the CEO of the merged entity. This was indeed a generous offer.

Deep down, I was not convinced about the sentiment behind the merger. Real estate, at the end of the day, is a regional business. This is because each state controls its land and therefore, the laws vary from place to place. And each city has its own market dynamics. So it is difficult to become a pan-India player.

Many Delhi developers who had expanded into markets like Mumbai and Bangalore burnt their fingers and exited most of their projects. This is why builders are happy developing in just one state and seldom venture out of cities.

While the talk of the merger was still in its initial stages, sometime in early 2014, Preety Kumar, the managing partner of Amrop, a global executive search company, called me to find out if I would be interested in a new assignment.

My first reaction was to decline the offer. This was because she wasn't prepared to disclose the identity of the company that had given her the mandate. Though I had an open mind regarding the subject, I was not desperate to find another job. I am also a firm believer that such decisions should never be taken in haste.

I soon forgot about the offer. A month or so later, I received another call from her. This time I decided to play along—just out of curiosity.

We agreed to meet in her office in Global Business Park, Gurgaon. She still hadn't shared the identity of the company with me. It was only when we met, that she disclosed that it was the Bharti Group led by Sunil Bharti Mittal.

All I knew about Mittal was that he was the poster boy of the Indian telecom revolution, a sterling self-made businessman and a philanthropist of substance—his Bharti Foundation, which works primarily in the area of education and sanitation, has a corpus fund of Rs. 200 crore.

Within twenty years of starting operations, Bharti Airtel had become the largest provider of mobile telephone services in the country, with over 250 million subscribers. It ended 2013–14 with a consolidated turnover of over $14 billion and a profit (before tax) of $1.3 billion. The story of his rise was truly amazing.

His father, Satpaul Mittal, was not a businessman but a politician, a member of the Congress party. Sunil Mittal, his second son, was born in 1957. The family lived in Ludhiana where the tradition of entrepreneurship is strong, supported by the availability of a large base of skilled manpower.

Mittal got into business at the age of eighteen, even before he had finished college. He started a small factory to make bicycle parts with the Rs. 20,000 he had borrowed from his father.

In 1980, Mittal sold the cycle parts business and relocated to Mumbai and started afresh as a trader of imported stainless steel, brass, plastics and zip fasteners. Business would take him to various parts of the country.

According to one account, while he was on a visit to Delhi, he had gone to Bengali Market—a popular place known for its Indian fast food joints. There, Mittal happened to meet a harried salesman for Suzuki's generator sets. He had been sent by the Japanese company to appoint dealers in India.

Suzuki had assumed that, like in Japan, people here too would buy its portable generators to use in ice-cream vans, hotdog trucks and exhibition kiosks. The salesman soon discovered that there was no demand for these generators from the intended customer base.

However, Mittal realized quickly that these generator sets could be sold to shops, small offices and even houses because of the frequent power cuts. He spoke to the salesman, and was soon appointed as the first dealer of Suzuki's portable generators in the country. The business met with instant success.

This whetted his appetite further. At a trade fair in Taiwan, he saw, for the first time in his life, push-button telephones. Indians were still using clunky, heavy old phones that came with a rotary dial. There was, of course, no way you could speed-dial or redial the number on these phones. All instruments were made by the state-owned Indian Telephone Industries (set up immediately after Independence).

Mittal knew instantly that push-button phones would be hugely successful in India. Within days, he had signed a contract with a Taiwanese supplier.

That was his entry into the telecom sector. Soon, he got a licence to make phones, which he sold under the Beetel brand. And when the government opened up mobile phone services, Mittal too jumped on the bandwagon and got the licence for Delhi. He launched services under the Airtel brand. His success is the stuff that legends are made of.

From there, he expanded to the rest of India and then to markets like Sri Lanka and Bangladesh. He later acquired Zain's African assets for $10.7 billion. He became a regular in all the global lists of multi-billionaires across the world.

In spite of these successes, the spirit of entrepreneurship stayed with him. He frequently forayed into new areas, though not always to great success. He ventured into insurance with Axa, wholesale trade with Walmart, FMCG with Del Monte and agriculture with the Rothschild family. He had even thought of getting into the airport business.

Little did I know that he had a fairly large real estate portfolio as well, which he was keen to increase! Preety Kumar, in the course of our first meeting, told me all about it.

I was impressed. And being a part of the Mittal business empire meant not being starved of growth capital.

But there was a hitch. I had a stake in Alpha G Corp, which, in a way, represented my life's savings, and was waiting for the company to get listed in order to monetize that stake. But given the adverse investor sentiment, especially in real estate, I saw little hope of that happening.

I would join, I told her, only if Sunil Mittal agreed to purchase my stake in the company. She promised to get back to me with regard to my demand.

In a few days, I heard from Kumar again. She said my 3 per cent stake in Alpha G Corp was too small to get Sunil Mittal interested. I understood—a businessman of his stature could not be seen as just a 3 per cent shareholder in Alpha G Corp.

That, for me, was the end of the matter. So I was surprised when, a month or so later, she called again and requested me to meet the Bharti Group's human resources director, Inder Walia, and its finance director, Sarabjit Dhillon.

I said I was okay for a chat but not a job interview. She agreed.

We had a casual meeting in which Walia explained the whole structure of the Bharti Group, and suggested I meet Sunil Mittal. I was still not very convinced. When Kumar called to fix up my meeting with Sunil Mittal, I agreed. More than anything else, I saw this as an opportunity to meet Mittal, one of the sharpest minds in Indian business.

My appointment with him was fixed: I was asked to meet him at 4.30 p.m. in his office in Vasant Kunj, in south Delhi.

The meeting was supposed to last fifteen minutes—it went on for an hour-and-a-half. He told me his story, right from the very beginning. Real estate, he said, was his first love and telecom just happened on its own. He had personally consolidated land at Faridabad and Gurgaon, including 100 acres in DLF Qutab Enclave in Gurgaon, but couldn't take it forward. This had educated him about the nitty-gritties of the business.

I found his knowledge of the various processes quite extensive. He was not just another businessman with some extra cash, which he wanted to park in real estate. His insights were precise and accurate. I began to feel that working with him would be enjoyable.

I then told him the story of my life and shared my experiences over the last three decades with him. I also told him that real estate was not a business of hierarchy—it required entrepreneurship. That's why large business houses had failed to make it big in this sector.

Mittal concurred with me. It was clear that we had struck a common chord. By the end of the interview, we were talking in Punjabi! He said it was a great match and that I should join him right away.

I too was taken in by his straightforward ways and his considerable charm. I ended up telling him that I had told Kumar that I had agreed to meet him only to see what he was like face-to-face. I also told him about my stake in Alpha G Corp and the need to find a solution to the problem.

Mittal, to his credit, was amused by my admission and promised to look into the matter of my stake.

In a few days, he had worked out a structure for me. What he proposed was truly interesting. I would be the managing director of Bharti Realty, the real estate arm of Bharti Enterprises, which is the holding company for Bharti Airtel.

It would house all assets that yield regular rentals. It was not a small company. It had a substantial rental income, and my mandate was to ramp it up further in five years' time. In addition, we would incubate a new company called Bharti Land, which would look at other projects like residential projects. It would do joint ventures as well as real estate asset management. This company had an entrepreneurial element to it, and Mittal offered me a stake in it. It would be my job to drive this company too.

This was too good an offer for me to turn down. Two factors appealed to me. One, the Bharti brand had huge equity in the market which could be leveraged for growth. The world has for long debated the intrinsic worth of telecom brands: mega brands tend to die once the ownership of the operating company changes. For example, in India, Hutch was a huge brand into which a huge amount of money and effort was invested. But once the business was acquired by Vodafone, it had to make way for the British telecom brand. Not for nothing do some experts find telecom brands a mile wide but only an inch deep.

However, Bharti Airtel had managed to connect with the market. One survey showed it is the most powerful Indian brand after the state-owned Life Insurance Corporation. People had come to associate it with reliability and innovation.

The second factor that played on mind was that Bharti was a large group with robust finances. Though some analysts have often commented on the huge debt in the Bharti Airtel's books, contracted on account of the Zain acquisition and spectrum auctions, it is a very well-managed and efficient, and hence, a profitable company.

I decided to say yes to the offer. There was really no sane reason for me to decline.

All hell broke loose when I announced this at Alpha G Corp.

I knew it was never going to be easy. After all, I had worked with Ghanshyam Sheth for twenty-one years and with the Choudhrie family for eleven years. These relationships had very strong roots, both professionally and personally. But there comes a time in life when a person has no option but to take a leap of faith.

The initial reaction, as expected, was a vehement no. 'We are like family,' I was told. 'If you have anything in your mind, you just have to say it.'

Of course, it must have been playing on their minds that my exit could destabilize the company. I was looking after its day-to-day affairs. For the market too, I was the face of the company.

It must be said that Sheth and the Choudhrie family had given me total freedom to run the business, and I had displayed total ownership over the company. Separation, therefore, was never going to be painless.

I decided to meet each of them individually before I departed from Alpha G Corp.

I met Sheth at the Willingdon Sports Club in Tardeo, Mumbai, in June 2014 for close to three hours, during which I poured my heart out to him. I listed all my concerns, but emphasized that I cherished the time I had spent with him. I convinced him that I wasn't there to negotiate better terms with him, and that the people below me at Alpha G Corp should also get the opportunity to grow.

Sheth, ever the considerate man, saw my point. He agreed to let me go, but asked me to serve for one more year with the company. He probably needed that time to find a successor.

It then struck me how Indian corporations never seemed to be invested in succession planning. One person decides to leave and the whole ship looks shaky. That's the reason why a changeover at the top is seldom smooth. Not just in the corporate sector, in other fields too, like politics and cricket, hardly any attention is paid to this crucial aspect. Under ideal circumstances, a second rung of command should always be in place in case the leader decides to quit all of a sudden.

Anyway, I told Sheth that one year was too long. If a person has decided to move on, he switches off from the present job and productivity falls, which is not good for the organization. I offered to stay on for three months, during which I would groom my successor.

In addition, I promised that I wouldn't take a single day off during this period. I also assured him that even after I left Alpha G Corp, I would, in whatever way possible, work towards the best interests of the company. After all, I owned 3 per cent of the organization.

I also met Sudhir Choudhrie four or five times. He had always been very fond of me and as a result, I always had direct access to him. With him too, my relationship extended well beyond the professional sphere. When my daughter, Aayushi, got married in February 2012, he had ensured that his entire family flew down from London to attend the functions.

It was never going to be easy for me to tell him that I wanted to exit Alpha G Corp and he made it amply clear that my decision had hurt him. I had to assure him that this was a professional move and it was never my intention to cause him pain. But one has to move on.

In August 2014, I joined Bharti Realty.

The press release issued with regard to my appointment said I was joining for 'conceptualizing and implementing a scalable business strategy and providing overall leadership to the business'.

For Bharti Enterprises, the real estate arm was initially meant only to take care of the needs of the group. All the offices of the organization located in and around Delhi belonged to Bharti Realty.

My mandate was to increase the rental income and explore the opportunities in the entire spectrum of real estate activities: residential, commercial and mixed use (commercial as well as entertainment). By the time I came on board, Bharti Realty had delivered 2 million square feet of space in Delhi and its suburbs, while another 3.5 million square feet were under construction.

In commercial real estate, Bharti Realty's showpiece project was Worldmark, a high-end office-cum-retail project in Delhi's Aerocity, which offers a whopping 1.5 million square feet of space. It also launched its first mall, The Pavilion, in Ludhiana. In Kolkata, it was setting up a mixed use project.

My vision was to make Bharti Realty the most admired company in the real estate business, whose focus was on transparency, high ethics and care for customers. Bharti Land too held tremendous potential. It would give me the opportunity to implement my real estate asset management model, which I had conceived and fine-tuned at Alpha G Corp.

My joining Bharti Realty was not the end of my family's long association with Alpha G Corp. My second child, Ankush, who was born in October 1991, had right from his childhood shown an inclination for engineering and real estate.

After his education, he wanted to set up a real estate platform which would be akin to McKinsey in business management. The

Sheth and Choudhrie families were keen to get him on board. Some connections are made for life.

In 2015, Alpha G Corp was acquired by a US major private equity fund, Blackstone.

7

From Unorganized to Organized

The entry of Bharti Enterprises into the real estate sector was a clear indication that the winds of change had started to blow.

Once news of Bharti Realty's inception was out, offers began to come to us thick and fast. For these builders, the first option was to sell their project to us. If that didn't work out, they were looking at entering partnerships. This way, they could establish a credible name that would help sell the project. We were approached by several middlemen, especially international property consultants. It was clear that their business has increased manifold in this market.

One day, we were approached by executives from Jones Lang Lasalle. They told us that one of their clients was talking to large corporations, including Tata Housing and Godrej, but wanted to go ahead with us because of our strong brand equity in north India.

The developer was Eros Group. With over sixty years of experience in the national capital region, it had built well-known townships like Charmwood Village, Eros Garden and the Lakewood City in the southern suburbs of Delhi, and Rosewood City on the Gurgaon–Sohna Road, theatres like Vishal Cineplex in Rajouri Garden and Eros One in Jangpura, business centres like the International Trade Tower, American Plaza, and Eros Corporate Tower in Nehru Place, and Eros Corporate Park at Gurgaon, and hotels like Eros Hotel at Nehru Place, Shangri La Eros at Ashoka Road and Double Tree by Hilton at Mayur Vihar.

Eros was among the better lot of developers in and around Delhi, yet the slowdown had impacted its businesses. It had a residential project coming up in Surajkund. Raman Sood, the managing director of Eros Group, wanted to sell the project to us, but we declined to take up his offer. Instead, we said, we would enter a collaboration: while the land would be contributed by Eros Group, we would support the project in every other way. Whatever the revenue, we agreed to share it between us.

The first task for us was to get us enlisted as the developer of the project. Thankfully, the new Bharatiya Janata Party government in Haryana had made it mandatory in case of a joint development like this one to get all the parties enlisted by paying 25 per cent of the licence fee. Though this escalated the cost to an extent, it gave solid protection to the buyers. Earlier, landowners would sell their projects, and the developer would, at times, collect the money and vanish. When the buyers approached the government, the records would not have any mention of the developer. Thankfully, Haryana had plugged this gap.

The writing on the wall was clear: in a matter of years, real estate could become like other industries where organized corporate players would command the lion's share in the market.

Till not so long ago, big corporations chose to stay away from this sector due to the rampant corruption and the sheer number of cash transactions—a situation made worse by inadequate regulations.

Apart from Bharti, several other respectable business groups like Tata, Godrej and Mahindra too entered the real estate business. Some corporations which had factories in suburban areas realized that they were sitting on prime real estate—they too were ready to jump on the bandwagon.

In a short period of time, most of these corporations scaled up their real estate operations. Tata Housing, which was revived by Tata Sons in 2006, had interests in residential, commercial and retail segments of the market by 2015. It had land banks in Mumbai, Ahmedabad, Bangalore, Gurgaon, Chandigarh and Kolkata, and had said that it wanted to acquire more land across other cities too.

By the end of 2014, Tata Housing had residential projects totalling over 70 million square feet, ranging from low-cost homes to luxurious villas. For low-cost homes, the company set up a fully-owned subsidiary, Tata Value Homes, in 2010. In early 2015, it launched high-end flats in central Delhi, in the coveted Lutyens Zone, at Rs. 190 crore apiece.

Godrej Properties had under its belt real estate development of over 8 million square feet across twelve cities by 2015. Mahindra Lifespaces had completed projects of over 7.3 million square feet by the end of 2014, and had another 11.3 million square feet of ongoing and forthcoming projects. It had its Mahindra World City developments in Chennai and Jaipur, and its residential projects were located in Mumbai, Pune, Delhi–NCR, Nagpur, Hyderabad and Chennai.

Whenever we debated the future for the sector, it became more and more evident that the days of the small developers were numbered. Their credibility has decreased considerably over time. People were not willing to trust them with their hard-earned money.

Trust is a critical factor in business, especially in a sector like real estate where people often put their life's savings into one project. It is very difficult for a company, or a brand, to regain trust once it is lost. The only company that managed it successfully was Cadbury.

Many years ago, worms were found in some of its chocolate bars. The controversy snowballed and the company's sales were hit. To its credit, Cadbury launched a high-decibel advertisement campaign, featuring none other than Amitabh Bachchan, which helped restore confidence in the market. In very little time, it had regained the market share it had lost to rivals.

But such instances are rare. In most cases, companies are unable to repair the damage done to their reputation. Most of the builders I spoke to were aware of this trust deficit, but had no clue about how to address the situation.

This erosion of trust in conventional builders, some of whom were fly-by-night operators, gave reason and hope to business houses, especially those with a strong corporate image, to enter the sector. All the groups which decided to enter real estate had built a strong brand equity, especially in the eye of the customer, by delivering high-quality goods and services over several years and by strictly following ethical practices: Tata, Godrej, Mahindra and Bharti.

Another reason that encouraged corporations to enter the sector was the efforts made by the government to plug the regulatory gap.

Much of what ails the sector was sought to be addressed by the Real Estate (Regulation & Development) Bill, cleared by the United Progressive Alliance government in 2013.

The Bill sought to put a lid on the unsavoury practices prevalent in the sector. It clearly said that a builder cannot launch a product without all the requisite clearances; there needs to be standard definitions of super area, carpet area et cetera; there should be a model sale–purchase agreement; and all brokers need to register with the regulator.

It also said that builders need to keep 70 per cent of the money collected from sale in an escrow account, so that the money is used for developing the project and is not diverted elsewhere. The Bill also had stiff penalties for those builders who violate its provisions.

Instead of supporting it wholeheartedly, the builders only cautious welcomed the Bill. That's understandable as it sought to make builders solely responsible for any misdemeanour. That cannot happen as long as there is corruption at the ground level.

Builders overconstruct and cut corners because they need to pay hefty black money for every single clearance. By all means, hold them responsible, but only after making the whole process transparent and time-bound. If after they still indulge in unethical practices, then they should be taken to task.

However, before the Bill could be passed in Parliament, the United Progressive Alliance government fell. The National Democratic Alliance came into power based on its twin promises of growth and transparency. That gave hope that the Bill would be taken to its logical conclusion.

The way the government reformed the insurance, coal and mining sectors made everybody confident that real estate too would soon have a regulator. And the government started to look into the arguments put forward by the builders.

In April 2015, the Union Cabinet approved the Real Estate (Regulation & Development) Bill with three changes. These were well thought out and significantly improved the 2013 version of the Bill.

Thus, commercial real estate was brought under the ambit of the Bill. This was a welcome move. Malpractices abound in this segment of the real estate market as well, and there is a pressing need to pull up errant builders.

Two, the Bill said if a builder wants to alter the design or structure of the project, he will need to take the consent of at least two-thirds of the buyers. This seems to have been prompted by those cases where builders were found guilty by the courts of building extra floors on their own without telling the buyers.

And three, the Bill stipulated that builders will need to deposit 50 per cent of the money collected from the buyers in an escrow account, which will be used only for the project. In the earlier Bill, the proportion was 70 per cent. But after consultations with other stakeholders, especially builders, it was reduced to 50 per cent. This might not be a bad thing, given the high prices of land in the country.

The idea of the escrow account is to keep a check on serial builders who use the money raised for one project to buy more land and launch newer projects. By doing so, the builder ensures that the first project is inordinately delayed.

All these steps could restore investor confidence in the market. This coupled with the rising corporate interest augurs well for the future of the real estate sector.

Having a regulator is important. The next logical step ought to be to make the various processes involved in real estate transparent and non-discretionary. Many projects get delayed because of the sheer amount of red tape involved. Black money for various clearances is the norm in the sector. All of this adds to the cost of the builder, which he then extracts from unsuspecting buyers, or recovers by cutting corners. This had started to drive investors away from the sector.

However, this is the difficult part. Every state has a different set of rules and regulations for real estate. And 'contributions' from builders fund a large number of political campaigns. As a result, there is no urgency in any state to reform the sector. Now with a regulator in place, which will hopefully protect the interests of the investors, it is hoped the builders will put pressure on the states to introduce transparency. Unless this happens, real estate reform in the country will remain only a half-baked measure.

The election of Narendra Modi as prime minister in May 2014 gave some hope that this sector could be cleaned up over the next few years.

In September 2014, Modi said that he wanted India to be amongst the top 50 countries when it comes to ease of doing business (a month later, the World Bank, in its annual Doing Business report, gave India its worst ranking ever: 142 out of 189 countries). His biggest initiative in this direction was the move towards a uniform goods and services tax. Once the new tax is in place, it should take a consignment not more than three days to travel from Mumbai to Delhi—down from a week. Companies won't need to maintain warehouses in each state, and paperwork will reduce substantially.

Modi's message, thankfully, travelled down to the states. The new BJP government in Haryana, for instance, started to study how the processes for real estate could be made simpler and transparent. Others are bound to follow because states are now competing with each other to attract investments.

The only way to attract large corporations to invest in real estate is through reform. Those states which refuse to change will miss the bus—something they cannot afford to do now because the national debate has moved to growth and development. The BJP government in Maharashtra, for instance, cut by half the eighty or so approvals required to set up a factory in the state.

Maharashtra also became the first state in the country to have its own regulator for the housing sector: the Housing Regulatory Authority. The move was initiated by the earlier Congress–NCP government.

All developers in the state will have to register their projects with the regulator and disclose the status of the various clearances they are required to get, along with details of the construction costs, land records, deadlines and the registration applications. All of these will then be verified by the regulator.

Unless the developer has disclosed all this to the regulator, they cannot even advertise the project. Earlier, a prospective buyer found it impossible to get this sort of information from the developer.

In the new regime, all the buyer needs to do is check the website of the regulator. In case the courts declare the title deed invalid or invoke the power of attorney for the land, the registration of the project will be cancelled by the regulator and the developer will not be able to advertise or sell it. And in case the regulator is convinced that the developer cannot complete the project, the buyers can form a legal entity and complete it.

All real estate agents will also be required to register themselves with the regulator. This is significant because, in most cases, the buyer interacts with the agent who acts as the source for all the misinformation. They need to be reined in as well.

If this reform is carried out along with the easing of processes and ensuring all clearances are time-bound, it will provide a robust model for the other states.

With large corporations entering the sector, it is also possible that real estate will finally get the industry status, which it has been demanding for several years now. This will help it access funds from banks at a lower rate of interest.

Again, given the Modi-led government's growth agenda, this looks possible. He was voted to power on hopes of increasing growth and development, after economic activity slumped during the final years of the United Progressive Alliance government.

If his government fails to provide jobs to the country's young population—60 per cent of Indians are below the age of thirty— it will be voted out of power in the next general elections. The good thing is that the government seems fully aware of it.

Farming cannot handle any more people entering the sector. Farm sizes are becoming smaller, which can make farming uneconomical. At the same time, everybody cannot be provided a job in the services sector, the largest component of the Indian economy. Those who live in villages and are not highly educated or computer-literate will not find it easy to enter the sector.

That leaves manufacturing. And the government is trying to give it a much needed boost, as seen in its Make in India campaign.

But manufacturing is a complex sector, and its success or failure depends on a host of extraneous factors. Businessmen will invest in the sector only when it is economical to manufacture in India. In these days of a borderless world, investment tends to flow into regions that are most competitive. So, India has to not only look towards China, but also countries like Thailand, Vietnam and Malaysia to attract global capital.

I know several businessmen who have moved investments from India to Thailand, Vietnam and even Bangladesh because it is easier to do business there.

On the other hand, real estate has no such issues. Studies suggest that real estate can spur the growth in almost 300 other sectors. This is the reason why income tax sops were offered by the government several years ago to boost housing.

Some economists argue that sector-specific incentives do not work because they cause an imbalance in the allocation of the scarce resources. But India is at a delicate stage in its growth. These incentives can play a significant role in giving an impetus to growth and providing jobs to the millions of unemployed people in the country.

Real estate is increasingly becoming a highly capital-intensive business. The market is in a deep freeze. Nothing is selling. Cash flows have come to an absolute standstill. Developers who had raised debts to expand are finding it difficult to repay the money. And this state of affairs is expected to continue for some more time. The inventories, in some markets, could take several years to get absorbed.

It has become increasingly clear that only those with deep pockets can survive in the business. In fact, there is evidence that several builders, as constrained as they felt, were negotiating to sell their assets. Those who raised debts from private sources at usurious rates of interest too have no option but to cede control one day. Many of these are likely to be picked up by large corporations.

In 2014 itself, it was evident that home buyers were happy to do business with established names in business—the large corporations. During Google's Great Online Shopping Festival in December 2014, Tata Housing sold 200 houses across its various projects in the country. In the 2013 edition of the shop-fest, it had sold fifty.

Most Indians buy one house during their lifetime. Luckier ones may buy two. Every purchase sees several visits to the site, and a thousand enquiries about the builder. Any broker will tell you that it takes at least three months for a home buyer to make up his mind.

That's only because people do not trust their builders. Every buyer asks himself the same set of questions a thousand times over: Will the builder run away with my life's savings? Will the home be delivered on time? Will he keep all the promises he made? Is the land title above board? Has he got all the clearances?

The buyer cannot be accused of being unnecessarily paranoid: errant builders have, over the years, done every kind of misdemeanour possible, which has shaken the buyer's confidence.

Several have simply vanished with the money they collect from hapless buyers. Most have delayed projects extensively. Almost all have played around with the carpet area, floor area and super area to dupe the unsuspecting buyers.

The volume of realty bought online shows that there is some trust in real estate now. Of course, the entry of the Tata brand in the sector also helped. This is a strong signal that things could change for the better.

Of course, only those corporations with a strong brand value will be able to sell online, at least in the initial days. I don't think all builders will be able to sell realty online. Only those names which evoke a strong sense of trust will be able to do so.

However, the internet has emerged as a major tool in the hands of buyers to help research projects and to reach out to developers. According to a *Business Standard* report in January 2015, about 70 per cent of Tata Housing's customers reached out to the company through the internet.

A study done by Google said that between 2010 and 2014, real estate transactions worth $43 billion, or over Rs. 2,50,000 crore, were influenced by research done on the internet. Portals like Commonfloor, Housing and PropTiger had become extremely handy research tools to buy, sell and lease properties. Many of these portals have even received private equity funding at fancy valuations.

The online property sites have so far only dealt with listings. They are yet to work on all the transactions while buying property: payment, documentation, registration et cetera. The good thing is that it is entirely possible to do these transactions online. What is required is a platform that rates developers, provides links to legal experts who will ensure that all documentation is in order and all compliances have been received, provides access to banks for finance and even the state authorities for registration.

The good thing is that many state governments have digitized their records, so you can access these papers very easily. Once all this is done, a person sitting in Kolkata can buy a property in Delhi with just a click of the mouse.

The only hitch is: will people be comfortable making such high-value transactions online? Admittedly, this is a challenge. But I feel quite encouraged by the recent trends. For instance, a lot of people book their expensive overseas holidays, from business class tickets to hotel rooms, online. Indians are getting more familiarized with electronic banking. So the day when payments for real estate are made online is not far away.

At times, I do feel that our idea of Property Exchange would have been a hit in the current circumstances, especially since the title papers of all properties would have been certified by us. That would have enabled even smaller builders to sell property online. It would have received huge support from the buyers too.

Though the internet was just a medium for us to deliver the service, we were mistakenly, and unfairly, bracketed with other dotcoms—and therefore, no one was willing to invest in us. In hindsight, it was an idea much ahead of its time. But I am happy to note that my son now wants to revive the idea and take it forward.

There are plenty of indications that, very soon, real estate will become like any other sector of the economy where large corporations will play a defining role. The question is, where will this leave the small builders? What will happen to the huge amounts of money locked in their ventures?

Many of these builders could soon be driven out of business. Some may get acquired by larger organizations. This would also help these bigger corporations enter the sector. The returns may fall from 100 per cent to 18-20 per cent, but the business will be predictable and transparent.

Most builders, especially those who want to construct integrated townships, need to employ land aggregators. When I spoke to them in 2014, they complained that their payments were stuck with the builders. In almost all cases, the culprit was a small builder who had tried to overreach and was now in dire straits.

Many of these land aggregators would prefer to work with large corporations, which guarantee their payments.

But this does not mean that every large corporation that enters real estate will succeed. The Jaypee Group, which had interests in construction, cement, power and hospitality, entered the real estate market in Noida and Greater Noida in a big way. It also built, at a substantial cost, the Buddh International Circuit in Greater Noida and the Yamuna Expressway that links Agra and Delhi.

A large chunk of these investments were financed through debt. Analysts cautioned that the company had spread itself too thin by borrowing too much. Perhaps it was banking on the real estate projects to generate cash flow to pay off the debt. But, unfortunately, that's not how it played out. Once the real estate market collapsed and sales came to a grinding halt, the group faced a massive debt without adequate cash flows to service it. Finally, the company had no option but to sell several assets in order to reduce its debt. In the space of a year or so, it had to sell several of its cement and power companies—it was one of the biggest downsizing exercises in India's corporate world.

When the Modi government took over, some were hopeful that the sentiment in the real estate market would turn immediately. But unless the stockpile of inventory gets cleared, there is little hope for the sector. And this can happen only if the economy grows at a very fast rate over the next three or four years.

The good thing is, many global estimates have already claimed that India is on a revival mode. In 2015, for the first time in many years, India was projected to grow even faster than China. Even before he became the prime minister, Modi had talked about smart cities, which gave a whole new spin to real estate development in the country. After his government came to power, it announced its plans to create 100 smart cities.

Many wondered if the government would go through with its plan and actually set up 100 new cities. Post-Independence, only a handful of new cities have been established: Chandigarh, New Raipur (incomplete) and Lavasa (work in progress).

It is unreasonable to expect the Centre to set up 100 new cities in five, or even ten, years. Instead, Modi's plan was to turn 100 cities into smart cities.

What exactly is a smart city? In simple terms, it is one which uses information technology to deliver various services to its citizens: transport, healthcare, power et cetera.

The concept goes all the way back to 2008, when the Western world was in the grips of the economic slowdown. IBM, the technology giant, came out with a campaign called Smarter Planet. A vital component of that campaign was smart cities. Information technology was to be the principal infrastructure of such a city. Managing traffic on the roads, power on the grid and water in the pipes would all be done remotely, using information technology.

All bills would be paid online, and all public information would be shared on the internet. Needless to say, such a city requires enough telecom bandwidth to support this technology.

The idea caught the whole world's attention, more so in emerging markets. Most of these countries were seeing an urban explosion as people migrated from villages to towns and cities in search of a better life. And since cities did not have adequate infrastructure to support this rise in population, filth and squalor was on the rise.

The demand for good-quality urban spaces was rising steadily but the resources were limited. This can be addressed through the judicious management of resources. And this is where information technology could play a critical role.

The idea of a smart city fired the imagination of planners in emerging markets. Countries like South Korea, United Arab Emirates and China began to invest heavily in this concept.

In India, the lead was taken by Modi after he became prime minister. It became an integral part of his plan to boost urban renewal.

However, over here a smart city connotes something else. Apart from a robust information technology backbone, it should have an efficient transport system, adequate power and water, essential services within reach, proper civic amenities like parking slots and facilities that are disabled-friendly. Traffic jams, congestion and the breakdown of services would not happen in such a city.

According to a report that appeared in *The Hindu* in January 2015, the proposed smart cities in the country include Kochi in Kerala, Ahmedabad in Gujarat, Aurangabad in Maharashtra, Manesar in the National Capital Region, Khushkhera in Rajasthan, Krishnapatnam in Andhra Pradesh and Tumkur in Karnataka.

'Many of these cities will include special investment regions or special economic zones with modified regulations and tax structures to make it attractive for foreign investors,' the report said. 'This is essential because much of the funding for these projects will have to come from private developers and from abroad.'

The best way for the government to go about its agenda is to promote smart communities. In fact, no developer should be allowed to construct projects that do not adhere to the rules of a smart city. For instance, Gurgaon One, which was developed by Alpha G Corp, can easily be converted into a smart community with minimal investment. It does have ramps for the disabled, adequate parking, slots for stores et cetera. All that needs to be done is link it with the city's infrastructure.

Golf Course Road in Gurgaon, which is on its way to becoming the most exciting stretch of land in the city, will have smart infrastructure complete with overbridges, cycling tracks, a metro rail and disabled-friendly features. All a residential community needs to do in order to become a smart community is to link itself to this infrastructure.

At Bharti Realty, we decided very early on to not do any construction that is not smart. All our buildings, whether residential or commercial, will be smart, efficient, and of global standards.

India is an emerging economy but is quickly racing towards the status of a developed country. I am sure we will be there by 2030. In the next fourteen years, we will see a massive technological leap. This will require some serious re-development of cities. Whatever is not working efficiently will have to make way for smarter constructions.

The all-important question here is: will an apartment in a smart community cost more? Many fear that builders might use this just as an excuse to raise prices. While this could happen, I don't think the cost of making a community smart is prohibitive. If a conventional gated community is selling for Rs. 5,000 a square foot, making it smart would raise its costs by not more than 5 per cent.

I am convinced buyers will be willing to pay this much extra to enjoy the benefits of living in a smart community. Anyway, most Indians pay for their houses in instalments. This extra cost, when spread over several years, will not really affect them.

One major prerequisite to a smart community is access to high-speed internet. People can then pay bills, access information, and do most of their chores online. All of this will also help reduce the congestion on the roads as people will no longer need to drive just to run an errand.

Like smart banking, it is an idea whose time has come. With net banking and ATMs coming up in every nook and cranny of the city, people need not go to the banks at all. For many, a visit to the bank happens maybe once in six months. Once upon a time, a weekly visit to the bank was unavoidable.

Will the advent of smart cities mark the end of low-cost homes? In 2009, when Tata Motors launched the inexpensive Nano car, builders were inspired to try their hand at low-cost housing.

Frugal engineering was the flavour of the season. People talked of no-frills motorcycles, airlines, hotels and even homes. But the whole exercise soon ran out of steam. First of all, low-cost cannot become low-quality. An easy way out to target the bottom end of the pyramid is to cut out the bells and whistles, strip off some features and package it as a low-cost product.

This is a flawed approach. Existing products, stripped off their features, are unlikely to work with customers. They are too evolved to be happy with something that is second best.

Innovation happened when Dhirubhai Ambani told his son, Mukesh, that only if he could price a call at less than the cost of a postcard would his mobile services business have a future. Or when Jack Welch set up call centres in Gurgaon to answer queries raised by General Electric customers in the US. Running such call centres in the US was expensive. He saved millions of dollars by moving these to low-cost India. It wasn't long before many others followed Welch's lead.

Another example was when the Board for Control of Cricket in India introduced club-format cricket with the inauguration of the Indian Premier League. Though many purists felt that it had destroyed the beauty of cricket, the league's popularity has only risen after its launch in 2008. There have been allegations of spot fixing and financial impropriety, but that has not dented its value. Such is its appeal that some overseas cricketers have even skipped their national tours to play in the Indian Premier League.

Innovation also happened when Tata Motors launched the Nano, a car priced at just Rs. 1 lakh, or when Tata Chemicals launched a low-cost water purifier called Swach. In fact, the Tata group has institutionalized this spirit by forming a separate innovation council. It encourages employees to create newer products, tolerates honest mistakes and removes the fear of ridicule in case of failure. Others like the Mahindra group too have tried this approach.

Not every low-cost innovation was successful. Capt. G.R. Gopinath started India's first low-cost airline, Air Deccan. He claimed he had all costs under control and had tapped all revenue streams. Amenities to staff and customers were cut, e-tickets were made the norm, and space in the aircraft was sold to advertisers. But the business turned out to be far more complex than what he imagined, and, therefore, Gopinath could not keep a lid on the losses. He eventually had to sell Air Deccan to Vijay Mallya.

But the mess he left behind was such that it was one of the key factors that drove Mallya's Kingfisher Airlines to bankruptcy in a few years. Such was the impact that the flamboyant Mallya, whom everybody used to call the 'king of good times', had to cede control of his flagship liquor business.

The message is simple: to make a successful product, one has to start from scratch with a fresh mindset.

The issue with low-cost houses was that most builders took a top-to-bottom approach. They looked at the normal costs they incurred and started to figure out what could be cut out.

Whatever was considered fanciful was thrown out: granite slabs in the kitchen, tiles in the bathroom et cetera.

This may reduce costs but the buyers would be far from happy. They would have to spend more money after buying the house to do it up. This would put them back on square one.

Nobody took the reverse approach. Had somebody started from the bottom and used new materials and designs to build a house at reduced costs, maybe a proper solution would have emerged.

Budget hotels, for instance, have successfully brought down their building costs by viewing their construction from a totally fresh perspective. For instance, they are usually located away from the downtown areas or the central business district, which keeps their land costs low. Their rooms are identical—they call it the cookie-cutter approach. They work on a larger scale and with global vendors, which helps them buy raw materials and equipment at low costs. All unnecessary frills are done away with. The staff is asked to multitask: it is not surprising to see the receptionist also manning the bar!

Unfortunately, everybody looked for the easy way out while developing low-cost housing. Cutting costs here and there was passed off as 'fresh ideas'. But that is not to say that the sector has been bereft of innovation.

The biggest example of innovation in the real sector is the skyscraper, which was made possible by the invention of the elevator. Height was no longer a deterrent. Similarly, when we came out with the concept of real estate asset management, it was nothing short of revolutionary—it was now possible to enter the sector with a very small capital base.

We often associate innovation with a product or a process. Merely tinkering with a product or modifying the process is often lauded as 'innovation'. But, in the fast-moving times that we live in, this isn't enough. In the broader sense, the term has come to mean a change in the business model itself. Low-cost housing surely was a good idea. There is no debate about that. The poor too have the right to live with dignity and in proper, hygienic conditions. The problem is that land prices have become so high that no builder can hope to recover his costs by just building low-cost houses.

Moreover, getting all clearances for construction easily takes up to two years. During this period, the large investment in land sits idle, increasing the cost. This prompts the builders to opt for high-end apartments where they can charge a premium to help recover their investment.

In Gurgaon, for instance, few builders want to build houses for the economically weaker sections of society. It's not that the government is totally oblivious to their plight—the Haryana Apartment Owners Act of 1983 says that all builders have to construct 15 per cent of the sanctioned apartments for low-income buyers and another 10 per cent for the service staff.

So, if a builder is constructing a 300-apartment complex, he needs to develop another forty-five for the poor and thirty for the service staff, which are to be allotted by the government.

Clearly, these numbers are grossly inadequate. Most homes have at least one domestic help. In the tonier sections of the city, you may find up to seven helps in one house. Some of them live in the servant's room in the flat, but a large chunk of this population has to fend for itself.

Even the rules regarding such homes are openly flouted. Many builders who have built low-cost homes have chosen to locate them at a distance from the premium housing project. The result is that they are not integrated with the main condominium.

There have also been instances of owners using these residences for commercial activity. These houses are also of little use to migrants as they can be allotted only to below poverty line domiciles of Haryana.

The only places where land prices are low enough to construct such houses are the towns at a distance of 30–40 km from Gurgaon. But the lack of connectivity has acted as a major obstacle to developing this idea.

One way out of this problem is to enter a public–private partnership: Let the government acquire the land and hand it over to builders to develop low-cost apartments. But the Land Acquisition Act has made this difficult by pushing up the land prices.

Such lack of foresight has had some dire consequences.

All told, there are about 2,00,000 migrant workers who live in and around Gurgaon. These numbers are guesstimates: the authorities don't know the exact size of this floating population.

A July 2014 *Business Standard* report said that after the Ministry of Housing and Poverty Alleviation pointed out that there is a high percentage (approximately 28 per cent) of uncanvassed households in urban areas, the Municipal Corporation of Gurgaon started a survey of slum clusters. The report added that apart from Nathupur, there are two other large slum clusters that host the support staff of Gurgaon: Chhatarpur and Sikanderpur in Delhi. Slums have also come up near many of the 291 villages that fall within the city limits. Since the villagers don't let them squat on their land, they build makeshift homes wherever they can.

The sector needs larger players with a holistic view of development. Builders with a narrow worldview will only add to the mess. This is why the entry of large corporations needs to be welcomed.

Once this happens, real estate will finally get the respect it deserves.

Epilogue

Buying and Investing Mantras

In the last few years, I have seen a definite shift in the mindset of people. When the market was booming, people would come up to me at parties to know where they should buy property. Real estate values were on the rise across the country: residential as well as commercial. Some cities offered a lot more in terms of infrastructure, just like some builders commanded a premium. I was often asked which city, and which builder, would fetch the best returns.

After 2013, the question turned to: should I invest in real estate at all? Or, when will my real estate investments start appreciating?

Irrational exuberance has given way to utter despondence. Like extreme weather, extreme views on real estate are not desirable. What people forget is that like any other commodity, real estate must also go through a product life cycle. The problem is, when the cycle is on the upswing, nobody wants to believe it will come down, and once it is down, people think it will stay this way forever.

Investments are made for the long-term as well as the short-term. In the long term, the returns across asset categories—stocks, bullion and real estate—tend to converge. That's why most high net worth individuals prefer to park their long-term investments equally across these three categories. For them, the current pause in real estate does not make much of a difference.

For a long time, economists as well as analysts have tried to study the correlation between the three asset classes. It is complex, to say the least. When the stock indices are on the rise, investors pull money out of gold and real estate, and put it into the market. However, once they feel the stock market has plateaued, they might liquidate their holdings and invest the money in gold and real estate.

Real estate yields can be divided into two parts: rental income and capital appreciation. In this sense, real estate is different from bullion, where you only make capital gains. But this could change with the government initiating a gold monetization scheme, where people can keep their gold in a bank and gain interest, which could be in cash or in gold. But, there are some reservations about how this scheme will work.

In character, real estate is like stocks, where you get both dividend income and capital gains.

In good times, a rental income of 5 per cent (of the capital value) plus a capital gain of 10 per cent fetched an annual return of 15 per cent (inclusive of inflation), which means the value of your investment could double in six years or so. As years went by, the capital gains were even higher. It was not uncommon for people to double their investments in a matter of two to three years.

From 2013 onwards, however, the scenario changed beyond recognition. Rental incomes have fallen to as low as 1 or 2 per cent, while capital appreciation is more or less flat. This has made real estate lag behind the traditional asset classes. Even fixed deposits from banks fetch better returns. This is why builders are finding it difficult to sell their stocks.

The question is, when will the market turn? If you were to look at major markets, you will find that they are sitting on a huge inventory, something which will take years to clear. But in most of these markets there are segments which are doing well, where demand and supply are still evenly matched.

If you are an investor with a medium-term perspective of three to five years, it would be helpful to identify these segments. Look at the National Capital Region, for instance. While builders in Noida Extension, Greater Noida and Dwarka Expressway are finding it hard to sell what they have built, those in the more developed parts of Gurgaon face no such problems. Their sales continue to be brisk.

The reason is that many corporations have preferred to locate their offices in Gurgaon. Not only has this resulted in a strong demand for office space but has also boosted the demand for houses. In comparison, Dwarka Expressway, and for that matter Noida and Greater Noida, have not seen much favour with companies. As a result, these markets are suffering.

There is a very simple lesson to be learnt from this: go where the large corporations are going. The other thumb rule is: follow pockets of high activity. An example of this is Manesar, where there is a lot of industrial activity taking place. People generally prefer to live close to their place of work, provided it has basic facilities like schools and hospitals.

It is important to monitor such development. At one point in time, south Delhi used to be the most sought-after address for business houses. But once Gurgaon came up, the demand dropped dramatically.

Then, some years back, the Delhi Development Authority decided to reduce the minimum area required for a farmhouse from 2.5 acres to 1 acre. In one stroke, farmhouses became affordable to a bigger section of Delhi's population. Property dealers and consultants were inundated with queries from buyers.

The rush for farmhouses dented property prices in the private residential colonies in south Delhi. According to property dealers, prices crashed by as much as 25 per cent in the space of one year. People who could have bought a builder's flat in colonies like Greater Kailash, Green Park, Chittaranjan Park and Saket now realized that they could get a farmhouse for the same amount of money.

Investors had anticipated this policy change. Aware that such a decision would trigger a huge demand for farmhouses, they bought large swathes of land, which could then be developed into farmhouses, in and around Delhi. As a result, prices have more than doubled in the last few years in areas with good infrastructure for farmhouses: Chhattarpur, Rajokri, Bijwasan et cetera. The farmhouses in these areas could build multiple dwelling units.

There are over 250 villages in Delhi. The DDA had said that it would identify some villages on the 'green belt' as 'low-density residential areas' for the development of farmhouses. Or else, it was argued, that these villages would become slum clusters, ghettoes or unorganized colonies, much like Sainik Farms.

This meant that the DDA would develop the infrastructure and provide civic amenities in these villages. Hectic jockeying followed this announcement—investors tried convincing the authority to favour certain villages over the others.

Most observers felt it could take another three or four years for the infrastructure to come up. The development of social infrastructure, like hospitals, clubhouses and schools, could take even longer—perhaps up to ten years. In some villages, like Satbari, Asola and Chhattarpur in south Delhi, the infrastructure was already in place and hence, the new policy could come into effect soon.

It is also possible that some markets may buck the trend and behave differently from the rest of the country. For instance, while the economy was grappling with a slowdown, real estate in

West Bengal was buzzing: twenty-two new townships entailing an investment of Rs. 76,000 crore were announced in the state. This became possible after the Mamata Banerjee government, in 2014, restored the exemption for townships from the cap of twenty-four acres on land ownership it had imposed in 2011.

Starting 2013, a lot of people wanted to know if real estate prices had bottomed out or would they fall further? It is everybody's dream to enter the market when prices are at the lowest and exit when prices are at their highest—this can be seen across asset classes.

However, it seldom works this way.

The downslide of the last few years has been more like price correction than a crash. It is not as if builders have put up a garage sale of flats. Of course, brokers have had to pass on bigger discounts than in the past, but the difference is not huge.

Once in a while, builders put out offers that looked very attractive. Early in 2015, Supertech, at its Cape Town Project in Sector 74 in Noida, began to offer buyers free flats in Golf Village along the Yamuna Expressway. In Bangalore, Nitesh Estates offered heavy discounts on the purchase of some of its apartments. Earlier, the Lodha Group organized a flash sale at its Lodha Grandezza project in Thane—offering flats at roughly Rs. 8,000 per sq ft, down by more than Rs 3,000 per sq ft. In Kolkata, Siddha Group and Eden Realty gave away a free car on the purchase of a flat.

But such offers are few and far in between. Still, home buyers could use this opportunity to invest. It is unlikely that prices will soften substantially from here; hard negotiations will yield a handsome discount. But there are certain rules that you should always keep in mind:

1. Who is the builder? Look at his track record carefully. Has he delivered his earlier projects on time? Has he made changes

in the layout after you entered into an agreement with him? Has he added extra floors or done any extra construction, like a school without the consent of the buyers? If he has, he is obviously taking you for a ride. It is always a good idea to contact old customers and find out such background information about the builder. Do they speak well of him, or are they dissatisfied? What is the quality of the construction?

Nothing works better than word of mouth publicity. Never get carried away by fancy advertisements or film stars endorsing products.

If the builder is listed on the stock market, it is not difficult to find out the company's latest financial health. Even otherwise, all companies are require to file their financial statements with the Union Ministry of Corporate Affairs. These records are available online and can be accessed by paying a small fee. Builders that are financially overstretched should be avoided.

To a large extent, serial builders are responsible for the mess the sector is currently in. Before buying from them, make sure you know if they have delivered on their past promises.

2. Go for a builder with a strong corporate identity. Is the project, in which you propose to invest, important for the business house? Will its other businesses suffer if the project is delayed or exceeds the budget? You will always find that large groups, which guard their image zealously, do not dupe their customers because it erodes their brand equity and can impact their other businesses.

It helps in another way: large corporations, given their managerial bandwidth, are more likely to follow due processes than smaller companies. In real estate, it is essential to note if the land titles are clear and if the various clearances have been received. While smaller companies can be opaque, large corporations tend to be more process driven.

If you look at buying property online, it is best to restrict yourself to builders with strong corporate values. Their brand evokes trust, a large amount of which is required if you are buying a property online.

3. Read the contract carefully before signing it. Many builders make tall promises before you buy their flats, but when you read the fine print you realize that they cannot deliver on these commitments. Most of them play around cleverly with concepts like floor area, super area and carpet area. Be very sure of what you are buying. It is fashionable among builders to promise a penalty in case the project gets delayed, but it is laced with so much legalese that buyers seldom get that money. It is helpful to get lawyers to read the contract and help you understand the fine print.

4. Is the construction smart? Just like smart cities, there needs to be smart buildings. This means various things: It should have a proper system to back-up power and water supply, it should have smart elevators, it should conserve energy and recycle water, it should have modern processes for the disposal of solid waste, it should be disabled-friendly, and it should have an efficient communication system.

But don't let the builder charge a huge premium for these services. They actually don't cost that much. In an upscale gated community, it may raise the price by up to 5 per cent, but certainly not more than that. If a builder demands a bigger premium from you, put your foot down—he is trying to fool you. Don't fall for these tricks.

Some builders, including Bharti Realty, have decided not to construct anything that is not smart. In other words, smart buildings will become the norm, rather than the exception, in the times to come.

With regard to office space, there were clear signals by the middle of 2015 that things had started to change for the better. According to Colliers International's review of the Indian office property market in April 2015, 'the economy and the office market turned the corner in 2014 and are poised for further improvement in 2015. For the commercial real estate sector, 2015 witnessed a good start, with first quarter office absorption of 8.5 million square feet in the eight major metro cities in India, headed by Bengaluru (3.82 million square feet, including 1.74 million square feet pre-committed), NCR–Delhi, Gurgaon and Noida (1.48 million square feet), Mumbai (1.33 million square feet), Pune (0.89 million square feet), Chennai (0.81 million square feet) and Kolkata (0.22 million square feet).'

Giving reasons for the revival, the report said, 'The Indian economy continued to see positive trends, with Business Confidence Index marginally up by 20 basis points in January 2015. India's GDP recorded a 7.5 per cent growth in October–December 2014; and the forecast is for the GDP to expand by 7.8 per cent in the January-March 2015 quarter. In addition, the WPI (Wholesale Price Index) inflation reached its 10-year low at 2.06 per cent in February 2015.'

With the economy all set to pick up, the demand for office space is bound to see a sharp upswing in mid-2016. This growth will be driven by the information technology sector. I have watched with fascination the rise of the internet economy in the last couple of years. These are a talented bunch of youngsters who are devising mobile apps to run the whole world.

I see them evolving into big movers and shakers of the real estate market in the days to come. Again, the demand will be for smart offices—anything that is not smart will simply not sell. The reason is quite simple: most of these companies are staffed by very young people who don't think twice before switching jobs. This runs the risk of delaying, or even derailing, existing projects. Therefore, it is important to create loyalty among employees. And you can't do that without a smart office.

Take a look at all the technology companies: their offices are always funky and in touch with what the youth want. Careful thought goes into their design. For instance, in some companies, the work can get tedious. To keep the employees engaged, such offices come in handy. If an employee leaves, the company has to incur fresh expenditure by hiring and then training a new person. That's why smart and funky offices have become the norm now.

As far as malls are concerned, their future looks uncertain to me. E-commerce has dealt them a terrible blow.

Most of the e-retailers are flush with private equity. They are using this money for customer acquisition. As all of them are on growth mode and e-commerce is the flavour of the season, nobody has bothered to enquire about their profits. As long as the party continues, all will be well. But the day the funds run dry, one is not sure what will befall the sector.

People prefer buying things online because of how convenient the whole process is. Going to the market or a shopping mall is a huge hassle. In contrast, you can buy the same stuff sitting in the comfort of your home—and at a lower price. To be fair, the e-retailers have done some interesting innovations in India, like cash on delivery and free returns.

Unfortunately for brick and mortar stores, the foreign investment norms have turned unfavourable. While the government has allowed only 51 per cent foreign direct investment in multi-brand retail (most important of which is that the final decision is with the state), foreign money is flowing freely into e-retail.

Strictly, foreign investment is not allowed in e-commerce, but it is allowed in something called an online marketplace, which is essentially a trading platform. Thus, most e-retailers work as marketplaces. This has given them free access to foreign funding.

Till this matter gets sorted out, investors are advised to be cautious about investing in the retail space.

Overall, real estate remains a good investment in the long run. Sooner or later, the Indian economy is bound to pick up. By the middle of 2015, India emerged as the fastest growing large economy of the world, ahead of even China.

Once demand and supply are evenly matched, once strong corporations begin to play a dominant role in the sector, once a strong and active real estate regulator is introduced, and rules become transparent, this business will only move from strength to strength.

Index